Living in the Shadows of a Ghost

Living in the Shadows Of a Ghost

The Emotional Cost of Loving a Widower

Michele Withonel

First published 2026.

ISBN 978-1-7645345-0-5 (Paperback)

ISBN 978-1-7645345-1-2 (Ebook)

Published by Michele Withonel.

This book is a work of lived experience and personal reflection. The views expressed are those of the author and are not intended to replace professional advice. This book does not constitute medical, psychological, legal, or therapeutic guidance. Readers experiencing distress, grief, or emotional difficulty are encouraged to seek support from qualified professionals.

Acknowledgements

This book is shaped by the women who trusted me with their stories, the professionals and the researchers whose work helped guide my understanding and lit the path before me. To every woman who shared her truth, quietly, bravely, and with unfiltered honesty — your voices live within these pages.

I also honour the woman I once was. Her hope, her mistakes, and her courage brought me here.

This book is dedicated to the people who carried me through every chapter of this journey. To my children and grandchildren, your love, strength, and unwavering belief in me have been my anchor. And to my soul sister, whose wisdom walked beside me through grief, through sorrow, and back into the light more times than I can ever name.

This book exists because of you all.

Preface

There is a story rarely told of women who fall in love with widowers still living partly in the past. We're told to be patient, to understand, to wait. But no one warns us what it feels like to love someone who can't fully choose us because part of his heart still belongs elsewhere.

This book was born from my own story: a relationship that started in hope and ended in heartbreak. Along the way, I discovered countless women walking the same quiet, painful path.

If you've ever felt like a guest in your own relationship, invisible beside a memory, this book is for you. May it give you language for what you're feeling and permission to choose a love grounded in the present.

Table of Contents

Contents

Introduction

The modern dating landscape is challenging enough, but there is a specific kind of heartbreak that only women who have loved an unhealed widower truly understand. It is a quiet, disorienting pain, rarely spoken about, often dismissed, and rarely acknowledged in mainstream conversations about grief and relationships.

This book is for the women who stepped into love with openness and hope, only to find themselves confused, sidelined, or emotionally wounded by dynamics they never anticipated.

Before my relationship with a widower, I thought I understood the depths of grief. I had watched friends mourn their partners and experienced my own heartbreaking loss. Years earlier, I had loved a man I believed I would grow old with, only to lose him to cancer. So, when I met Bill five years later, I wasn't searching for love, or even open to the idea of it. Yet he arrived quietly, unexpectedly, and with a gentleness that felt strangely safe.

But when the emotional challenges specific to widower relationships began to surface, I didn't have a framework to understand what was happening. I didn't have the language to explain the confusion that began building inside me. And I didn't have anyone to turn to. Like many women in this situation, I began my journey feeling isolated, wondering if I was imagining things, or worse, if I was the problem.

Eventually, I discovered I wasn't alone at all. I found communities of women asking the same questions, carrying the same hurts, and navigating the same emotional contradictions. Their stories helped me understand mine, and from that shared understanding, this book was born. I wrote it so that no woman has to face these experiences without guidance or validation.

There is something important I must say up front, because too many women recognise this truth only in hindsight: A relationship with an unhealed widower comes with emotional terrain that simply does not exist in typical relationships. There are landmines tied to grief, guilt, memory, and identity, patterns that can leave even the strongest woman questioning herself.

The beginning of a relationship with an unhealed widower can feel like a spark, but you must understand the source of that spark before you step into it, or you risk being burnt by the *Widower's Fire*, a dynamic that burns brightly at first, only to shift dramatically once deeper grief surfaces.

Most literature about widowers focuses solely on *his* grief, *his* loss, and *his* emotional journey. Almost nothing addresses the woman who comes next, the one who tries to love him while he is still emotionally tethered to his past.

This book is for her. For every woman who has felt overshadowed not by a living rival, but by a memory.

In these pages, you will find:

- stories from women who have lived through this dynamic.
- insights from psychology, grief theory, and relationship patterns.
- guidance on early warning signs.
- suggestions for what to do when issues arise.
- the language to name what you're experiencing.
- tools to protect your emotional well-being.
- clarity about when to stay, when to step back, and when to walk away.

You deserve to walk into a relationship with open eyes, not confusion, not blind hope, and certainly not self-blame.

When a man introduces himself as a widower, he is telling you that part of his heart is still anchored in the past. A man who is ready to begin again considers and calls himself *single*. He is not living in yesterday. He is choosing tomorrow, and he is emotionally available to invite you into it.

Living in the Shadows of a Ghost is divided into four parts, each designed to offer clarity, compassion, and grounded guidance. All names have been changed to protect privacy, including the man I once loved, whom I call Bill. I use the term *late wife* throughout the book to describe a widower's deceased spouse or partner.

This book is honest and direct. It does not romanticise the experience of loving a man who is still emotionally entangled with his past. Instead, it offers truth, mine, and the truths of many women who have lived in the emotional gaps created by unresolved grief.

If you have ever felt unseen, unchosen, or overshadowed by a memory, this book is for you. You are not alone. I see you. Your story matters.

Part 1 - Grief and the Widower's Journey

In this part of the book, we will explore the widower's journey through grief, and what this journey may mean for his next relationship. Together, we'll confront some of the uncomfortable truths that can come with loving a man who has lost a spouse, including the painful feeling that a deceased woman may sometimes feel *more alive* in the relationship than you do. This book is not about pitying the unhealed widower; it's about understanding how unresolved pain can become someone else's trauma.

We'll also examine the idea of finding yourself in what can feel like a "three-way relationship," where some widowers not only keep space in their heart for their late wife or spouse, which is natural, but also *expect* their new partner to love and revere this woman almost as much as they did.

We'll investigate the various ways unhealed widowers may keep the memory of their late wife current and central. While remembrance can be an important part of healing, we'll discuss how these behaviours can sometimes cross into territory that keeps the relationship stuck in the past, rather than allowing space to nurture love in the present.

Finally, we'll highlight some red flags that may signal the widower you've fallen in love with is not yet emotionally ready to meet you halfway and explore why the *Widowers Fire* can burn their new partners.

Chapter 1 – Widowers and Self Identity

"He still introduced himself as 'her husband and calls her his wife."

"His profile still said 'widower' years later."

"I felt like his grief got to stay, but I had to wait outside."

Grief is a complex, deeply personal, and multifaceted experience, deeply intertwined with identity and emotional bonds. From my experience of being in a relationship with a widower, I came to understand that grief doesn't just express itself through sadness, it also reveals itself through responsibility, guilt, fear, and the slow reconstruction of a life that no longer resembles what came before.

When I first met Bill, he introduced himself as a widower. I didn't realise it at the time, but that was my first clue. When a man describes himself that way, he is telling you, often without meaning to, that a part of his heart is still anchored in the past. A man who is ready to begin again usually considers himself single. He is not living in yesterday; he is choosing tomorrow, and he is emotionally available enough to invite someone into it.

I missed that clue. And I missed the second clue, too. In the beginning of our relationship, Bill would often weave his late wife into our conversations, sharing stories, memories, and moments with a tenderness that was hard to ignore. Sometimes he spoke of her by her pet name, other times simply as "my wife." Looking back, he was showing me exactly where his heart still lived.

Being in a relationship with a widower was uncharted territory for me. I had no idea that the way he identified himself was not merely a title; it was a quiet red flag, signalling that he was still deeply attached to the life he had lost and not yet emotionally ready for the one unfolding before him.

Understanding the emotional terrain of a widower's grief is crucial if you are considering a relationship with him. Before you can assess his availability or readiness, you need to understand where he is in his grief journey.

Psychiatrist Elisabeth Kübler-Ross [1] famously outlined five stages of grief in her 1969 book *On Death and Dying*. These stages are *denial, anger, bargaining, depression*, and *acceptance*. These stages were never meant to be a rigid sequence, and modern grief researcher David Kessler [2] has expanded on Elisabeth's work. In his 2019 book *Finding Meaning: The Sixth Stage of Grief*, Kessler emphasises that healing often comes through finding purpose or meaning after loss, a stage many widowers may not reach for years, if ever. Kessler suggests that widowers usually experience the stages of grief differently from others who mourn [2].

- **Denial** may surface as excessive busyness, a reluctance to talk about their loss, or entering a new relationship too quickly as a distraction from pain.[1] [2]

- **Anger** may not be overt but can show up as irritability, defensiveness, or emotional withdrawal.[1] [2]

- **Bargaining** often carries guilt-laden thoughts such as, *"If only I had taken her to the doctor sooner,"* or *"I should have done more."* [1] [2]

- **Depression** may appear as emotional numbness, a loss of joy, or a deep sense that life will never feel whole again.[1] [2]

- **Acceptance** is not about *moving on* but about learning to integrate the loss into daily life in a way that allows for healing and forward movement. [1] [2]

Many of the women I've interviewed whose relationships with widowers ended shared a common thread: the man they loved still seemed caught in an active state of grief. They described patterns that echoed denial, anger, bargaining, depression, and only fleeting glimpses of acceptance. As grief expert David Kessler reminds us, *"Each person's grief is as unique as their fingerprint."* No two widowers experience loss in the same way. [2] For many, these stages are not linear but cyclical, repeating over time until their loss is accepted and they are emotionally ready to move forward.

Abel Keogh, author of *Dating a Widower*, underscores the importance of emotional readiness among widowers seeking to date again. He notes, "*Widowers who are ready to date don't pine for their late wife. They're not constantly talking about her or comparing every woman they date to her. They're ready to make someone else number one in their life*". [3]

Through discussions with many women, I've found that problems arise when women assume a man is ready to move forward just because he claims to be. Words mean little if his behaviour is still embedded in grief. Some signs that a widower may not be emotionally ready include:

- Frequent references to his late wife in everyday conversation.
- A home that resembles a shrine to the past.

- A reluctance to make plans for the future.
- Emotional detachment or avoidance of intimacy.

If he cannot offer you a relationship grounded in the present, you're not unkind for taking a step back or walking away; you're wise for recognising that love without emotional presence is a form of emotional absence.

Case Study - Jonathon

Jonathon has dated two of the women that I've interviewed; he lost his wife to illness five years ago. Since then, the way he introduces himself both in person and online has rarely excluded the fact that he is a widower. On his dating profile, for example, the very first line reads:

"Widower, father of two, learning to live again."

His social media bios follow the same pattern: *"Proud dad | Widower | Lover of coffee and music."* Even when joining local hobby groups or online forums unrelated to grief, Jonathon often prefaces his comments with *"As a widower…"* or mentions that he lost his wife.

When asked why, Jonathon says that describing himself as a widower isn't only about telling his story, it's about honouring his late wife's memory and explaining the journey that shaped him. For him, the label "widower" isn't a temporary phase but a central part of who he is. He feels that people should know about the loss because it explains his choices, his views on life, and his moments of vulnerability.

Yet over time, some people around Jonathon, particularly women he has dated, have noticed that this deep identification with being a widower seems to keep his life anchored in the past. Even in new romantic contexts, Jonathon's self-introductions almost always include a reference to his late wife. In conversations, he often draws connections between his current experiences and moments he shared with her.

Jonathon doesn't do this out of a lack of respect for the present; rather, it stems from a genuine fear of "erasing" his late wife's life. By telling everyone, even casual acquaintances or new romantic interests, he keeps her alive in his narrative. To him, the widower identity is proof of love and loss, but to those meeting him for the first time, it can sometimes overshadow who he is now, and who he could become beyond the grief.

Recognising the Red Flags

Jonathon's story illustrates a subtle but significant red flag in dating a widower: when grief begins to dominate the present self and social identity. Remembering a late spouse is healthy, yet when it dominates how he presents himself to others, it can overshadow the person he is today. For a new partner, this can feel like entering a relationship with a man whose emotional space is partially occupied by someone who is no longer alive. It may raise concerns about his readiness to form a fully present, equal partnership.

From a professional perspective, grief experts caution that while remembering a deceased spouse is healthy, an overemphasis can unintentionally hinder new connections. According to Dr Pauline Boss, unresolved loss can create "frozen grief," a state where the mourner maintains strong emotional bonds with the deceased that block full engagement with the present [9]. In Jonathon's case, his repeated self-identification as a widower, even in contexts unrelated to mourning, demonstrates how grief can become a defining lens through which he experiences the world, rather than one aspect of a broader identity.

Family Systems theory also provides insight into this dynamic [26]. When a widower continually references his late wife to friends, acquaintances, or new partners, it can create a form of emotional triangulation. By anchoring his identity to his late wife, he inadvertently enlists others to keep her memory alive. Staying in the past shifts focus away from the present and onto the past, potentially leaving new partners feeling secondary, unacknowledged, or subtly responsible for preserving someone else's memory [26].

Experts often highlight the importance of boundaries, self-awareness, and honest reflection: a healthy approach to grief allows the past to coexist with the present without dominating it. A widower who can honour his late wife's memory while maintaining focus on the present and future demonstrates emotional availability and the capacity to grow in a new relationship. On the other hand, if grief constantly takes centre stage, through stories, social media posts, or casual conversations, it can signal that he's still working through his loss rather than wholly embracing a life with someone new.

What to Remember

Grief doesn't end; it seems to evolve, and sometimes, the identities we build around grief can limit our future relationships. It's essential to recognise the difference between grief that honours the past and grief that anchors someone to it.

Chapter 2 – The Red Flags of Unhealed Grief

"We'd planned a weekend away, but then he'd cancelled because it was her birthday."

"He told me I'd never understand what they had."

"Everything felt conditional, as if I was allowed in only so far."

In this chapter, we further explore the red flags that may appear when a widower has not yet resolved his grief. The aim is not to criticise or assign blame, but to bring awareness to the difference between a relationship that is ready to grow and one that remains anchored in the past. Throughout the book, most chapters include short reflections titled "Recognising the Red Flags," which highlight patterns that can emerge when love meets unresolved loss. Here, these insights are brought together to offer a clear and compassionate guide for identifying early warning signs and protecting your emotional well-being.

There were many of these "unhealed widower" red flags in my own relationship with Bill. At the time, I had never dated a widower and often struggled to understand what was happening. I was happily single and not seeking a relationship when we met. Bill called himself a widower because his last partner had died, a distinction that initially seemed minor but, in retrospect, was my first red flag. The man I had loved before Bill's arrival had also passed, but I had never described myself as a widow.

A man truly ready for a new relationship usually identifies himself as single. A widower who continues to define himself by loss may still be emotionally tethered to the past. From my conversations with women whose relationships with widowers did not last, a consistent pattern emerged. Unhealed widowers often define themselves by their grief, and memories of their previous relationship dominate the early stages of the relationship.

Even at the start of a relationship, subtle signs may reveal whether a widower is emotionally ready to engage in the present. Conversations may circle back to the late wife—not only with fondness, but with a type of emotional loyalty that leaves little room for a new partner. Photos may still be proudly displayed, a wedding ring may never leave his finger, or emotional distance may feel like a wall you cannot climb. These early patterns—persistent attachment to the past, reluctance to integrate a new partner fully, and avoidance of discussions about the future—are experiences I first noticed with Bill and are echoed in the stories of many women.

According to the experts, red flags often appear in **emotional and relational** patterns [20], as well as **behavioural and environmental** cues [4]. Recognising these signs early is not about blame, it's about clarity and self-preservation. Awareness allows you to set boundaries, seek support, and make choices that prioritise your emotional health.

In my own experience, noticing these patterns, sometimes subtly, sometimes painfully, was the first step toward understanding that love can honour the past, but it cannot thrive if the past dominates the present. True intimacy requires emotional availability, openness, and the willingness to build something new in the present.

The Red Flags

Emotional Red Flags

- An ongoing attachment to his late wife, communicated through frequent stories.
- Emotional distance or avoidance, he may avoid talking about his feelings or shut down when intimacy deepens.
- Mood swings triggered by anniversaries, holidays, or reminders of the past.
- Difficulty expressing love or fully opening up emotionally.
- Feelings of guilt or discomfort about moving forward in a new relationship.

Relational Red Flags

- Comparing you to his late wife, directly or indirectly.
- Frequently, 'accidentally' calls you by his late wife's name.
- Uses "we" or "us" when referring to past experiences with her.
- Hesitates about commitment, living together, or public displays of affection.
- Allows family or friends to prioritise the late wife over your relationship.
- Relies on you to manage his grief or emotional needs.

Behavioural Red Flags

- Keeps excessive photos, mementos, or belongings of his late wife untouched.
- Avoids conversations about grief or dominates discussions with grief-related topics.

- Intimacy feels rushed, confusing, or serves to soothe his emotional pain rather than foster a genuine bond.
- Shows inconsistent affection or emotional withdrawal.

Environmental Red Flags

- Home or life feels dominated by reminders of his late wife.
- Past marriage heavily influences decisions about holidays, family, or finances.
- Hesitant to fully integrate you into family, social circles, or daily routines.

Recognising the red flags allows you to protect your emotional well-being and set boundaries before patterns become embedded.

Understanding the Red Flags

Many women enter relationships with widowers filled with hope, compassion, and the belief that love can heal. Yet, some women find themselves navigating confusion, unpredictability, and unresolved emotions. What begins as empathy for a man's loss can gradually shift into emotional uncertainty when his grief remains unresolved.

Psychologists such as J. William Worden [4] note that emotional withdrawal and inconsistency are common signs of unprocessed grief. A widower may appear physically present yet emotionally unavailable, leaving his partner caught in a painful limbo of hope and doubt. Grief experts further emphasise that when family and social pressures go unexamined, such as expectations to preserve the late wife's memory, they can prolong attachment to the past and prevent the new relationship from forming a secure foundation [16][17].

For many men, physical closeness is simply a standard way of expressing affection. Dr Susan J. Elliott [8] describes a pattern she calls *instrumental intimacy*, where physical intimacy serves a practical or emotional purpose rather than fostering genuine connection.

With unhealed widowers, this phenomenon is what we call the *Widower's Fire,* where widowers seek intimacy and the company of a new partner as a distraction from grief and emotional healing. In these cases, intimacy is used to manage unresolved grief and emotional pain rather than to nurture a genuine, reciprocal bond. For their partners, this can feel confusing and hollow, as moments of tenderness are often followed by withdrawal, avoidance, or emotional distance.

Women in these situations often feel like bystanders in their own relationships. An unhealed widower's decisions, priorities, and daily routines may be shaped more by the past than by shared choices in the present. Pauline Boss [12] describes this experience as *ambiguous loss*, when a partner is physically present but emotionally tethered to someone who is no longer alive. The result can be a relationship suspended between compassion and resentment, where the living partner longs to feel thoroughly chosen.

Recognising these red flags helps you determine whether the relationship is built on readiness for the future or anchored in unresolved attachment to the past. Awareness empowers you to set healthy boundaries, seek support, and make choices that honour both your emotional health and the integrity of the relationship.

Unprocessed grief often becomes a silent third presence, occupying emotional space, shaping conversations, and dimming connection. Love can honour the past, but it cannot thrive when it is ruled by it. True intimacy requires emotional availability, openness, and the willingness to build something new in the present.

Why We Ignore the Red Flags

Many of us approached our relationships with compassion, believing that our love would be enough. I thought my love for Bill would guide him forward, and I assumed that time would naturally bring clarity, but in doing so, I often silenced my own instincts and feelings of discomfort.

Many women tend to overlook red flags in widowers because empathy and hope can overshadow their own need for self-protection. When someone is grieving, it's easy to rationalise their behaviour as temporary or understandable, even when it creates patterns that are harmful to a new partner. Patience feels virtuous, and hope becomes a lens through which inconsistencies are minimised.

In my case, I ignored persistent signs that Bill was still living emotionally in the past. I overlooked repeated comparisons to his late wife, emotional unavailability, and a reluctance to integrate me fully into his life. Compassion and hope are powerful forces, but without awareness, they can blind us to warning signs that our partner may not be ready for a healthy, mutual relationship.

Case Study – Emily's Story

Emily began dating Fred, a widower who kept his late wife's belongings untouched. Over time, Emily wondered if Fred was still grieving and not ready for a relationship. She noticed more signs: emotional distance around anniversaries, reluctance to discuss plans for the future, and constant references to the past. She felt increasingly uncomfortable living among the untouched belongings, as if she were intruding into a space frozen in time.

Every room held reminders of Fred's late wife: photographs on every wall, wardrobes still brimming with her clothes, bathroom shelves stocked with her personal toiletries, and even the kitchen cupboards filled with out-of-date spices she loved to use. Emily tried, gently, to share how these untouched items made her feel like an outsider in his life, hoping he might understand her perspective and consider discussing changes together. Fred, however, was firm that nothing should be moved or discarded. To him, these belongings were sacred and needed to be preserved exactly as they were. He even suggested that Emily keep some of his late wife's belongings as an honourable gesture, expressing disappointment when she admitted she felt uncomfortable about his request. He refused to part with anything, including the ancient spices, leaving Emily feeling unsettled and confused.

Later, Emily discovered that a painting in the living room depicting a half-naked woman was an image of Fred's late wife, which heightened her discomfort. Over time, reflecting on these repeated red flags helped Emily understand that Fred's grief was unresolved. Recognising this allowed her to prioritise her own well-being, and she ultimately made the difficult but healthy decision to end the relationship.

Case Study - Sarah's Story

Sarah dated a widower, Tony, for thirteen months. Early on, she noticed that he frequently referred to his late wife in the present tense, using "we" and "us," and that he maintained a shrine in her memory and wore a necklace containing his late wife's ashes alongside her wedding ring. When Sarah expressed discomfort about these reminders, Tony would flip the conversation, accusing her of being insensitive or jealous.

Over time, Sarah realised this pattern prevented her from speaking openly about her feelings, highlighting how unresolved grief can sometimes blur the line between mourning and emotional manipulation. Sarah felt isolated, as friends often didn't fully understand her perspective. She sought out information about widowers and grief, only to find that most resources focused on supporting the widower rather than acknowledging the experiences of the new partner. She also reached out to a therapist, who was unfamiliar with widower dynamics, leaving her feeling even more unsettled.

When Sarah tried to discuss her struggles with Tony, he dismissed her feelings, telling her, "You don't know what it feels like to lose the love of your life." This response left her feeling hurt and misunderstood, prompting her to question her place in the relationship, especially since she believed he was the love of her life. Over time, Sarah began to internalise the problem, questioning her own thinking and feeling that she had lost touch with her sense of self.

As her distress grew, Tony suggested she might need medication to calm her anxiety, further invalidating her emotions. Despite these challenges, he remained affectionate, and they continued to be intimate, leaving Sarah conflicted and confused.

Sarah eventually discovered an online support group focused on the often-unspoken realities of being with an unhealed widower. For the first time, she felt seen; reading stories and supportive comments from others gave her a sense of relief. When she shared some of these insights with Tony, he disagreed, explaining that his grief support group taught that the new partner should honour his past.

For a long time, Sarah would cry herself to sleep, trapped in her thoughts, trying to understand something she could not fully grasp. Eventually, she recognised that she was sacrificing her mental health for a relationship that left her feeling isolated and unheard. She made the difficult but empowering decision to end the relationship, remembering that love is not meant to feel painful or confining.

Recognising the Red Flags

Emily and Sarah both learned the same painful truth: even when a widower cares for you, his late wife can still sit in the centre of his heart. They loved hard but always felt like they were standing off to the side, that he's here in the room, but emotionally, he's somewhere else entirely, still tied to a life that ended. Experts on continuing bonds and relational grief say it's healthy to remember someone who has died, as long as those memories don't swallow the relationship that exists now [17]. And as David Kessler puts it, *"Grief must find a place in your life where it can live but not run your life."* [2]

For many men, affection naturally comes through touch. There's nothing wrong with that. But Dr Susan J. Elliott describes something called *instrumental intimacy*, in which physical closeness meets a need or calms a fear, without building a real emotional bond

[11]. With widowers who haven't healed, this can twist into what I call *The Widower's Fire,* that sudden rush of passion driven not by love, but by the need to escape pain. It feels hot, intense, like he wants only you... until he pulls away again. For the woman, it becomes heartbreaking whiplash: closeness that disappears the moment the lights go out.

Sometimes, what feels like your relationship isn't really yours at all. Choices, routines, even little daily decisions, can end up shaped by her memory or by what the family expects, rather than by what you both actually want together. Seeing this clearly isn't about pointing fingers. It's about protecting yourself, understanding your own needs, and figuring out whether this relationship is truly ready for the present... or still caught in the past.

Questions to ask Yourself

It can be hard to tell when a widower's behaviour stems from grief, and when it's part of a deeper pattern that may be harmful to you. Ask yourself these questions honestly:

1. Does he consistently show little or no empathy for my feelings?
2. Does every issue somehow revolve around how it affects him, rather than "us"?
3. Does he idealise his late wife in ways that devalue me, rather than honour her memory?
4. Does he refuse to seek help or take responsibility for his actions?
5. Does he require constant admiration or reassurance?
6. Does he blame me when I feel hurt, instead of offering understanding or apologies?
7. Does he show charm in public but coldness or cruelty in private?
8. Does he become angry or withdraw when I set boundaries?

A single instance of any of these behaviours can happen to anyone under stress. But if you notice persistent patterns, it may be less about grief and more about traits that could hurt you emotionally.

Opening the Conversation

Recognising red flags is only the first step; the next is deciding whether and how to address them. Bringing up sensitive topics with a widower requires courage, emotional intelligence, and timing. The goal is not to accuse or fix him, but to open an honest chat about whether the relationship is truly mutual and emotionally present.

Recognising the red flags early gives you a chance to understand where you stand, and helps you to:

- **Set boundaries** to safeguard your emotional well-being.
- **Seek support** from friends, family, or professional counsellors.
- **Make choices** that prioritise your needs and well-being.

People who work with grief often say that silence doesn't protect a relationship; it slowly pushes the couple further apart. Talking about what hurts isn't easy, but it's usually where healing starts. When you can both name what feels unfair or lopsided, there's a chance to find your way back to each other.

If you're starting to feel invisible or like you're living in the shadow of his past, gently speaking up for yourself can make a difference. Using "I feel..." statements keeps the focus on your experience instead of blaming him. For example:

- *"I feel left out when everything goes back to memories of your late wife. I want us to build some memories that belong just to us."*
- *"I feel unsure about my place when every family tradition still centres on the way things used to be. Can we talk about how to create some new rituals together?"*
- *"When anniversaries come around, I see how painful they are for you, but I also struggle to*

- *know how to support you without feeling pushed away. Can we talk about that?"*
- *"I notice I sometimes feel like a guest in your home when reminders of your late wife dominate. Can we discuss ways to balance the past and present?"*
- *"I want to share special moments with you, but I also need to feel fully included. Can we find a way to honour both?"*

How he reacts in these moments says a lot. Is he able to show up for you, or is he still living more with her memory than with you? That's where so many women get stuck, torn between empathy for his loss and frustration that there's no room left for them.

You can respect the past. You can acknowledge his love for her. But a relationship can't breathe if you're always competing with a ghost. For real closeness to grow, he has to be emotionally here, willing to open up, to try, and to build a life that exists now, not only in what used to be.

What to Remember

Love can honour the past but cannot thrive if the past becomes the centre of the present relationship. Intimacy requires emotional presence and commitment, and not just physical company. If you think it's a red flag, or are wondering if it is, then it's probably a red flag.

Chapter 3 – The Widower's Fire

"I have huge trust issues now."

"It felt like there were three of us in the bed."

"The way he dumped me was cruel and made me feel cheap. I felt like an unpaid prostitute."

Women who fall in love with widowers often enter a relationship they didn't plan for. They're trying to build something new, while he is still tangled in a past he never chose to leave behind. For some men, the grief they refuse to face doesn't disappear; it shifts. It shows up in the bedroom. What looks like burning desire can actually be a desperate attempt to feel anything other than loss. The woman thinks she's being pulled closer, when really he's trying to outrun the silence.

This phenomenon, what I refer to as the *"Widower's Fire,"* describes the intense desire for closeness that follows loss, a flame fuelled by grief rather than genuine emotional readiness. Many women have found themselves burned by this fire, mistaking the heat of desire for the warmth of love.

The *Widower's Fire* can hit like a storm, intense, seductive, and completely overwhelming. For the widower, closeness can feel like a healing touch, temporarily easing emptiness, guilt, or sorrow, and giving the illusion of a real connection. But for the woman beside him, it often leaves a gnawing confusion. She wonders: *Is this love, or just a way for him to escape the grief he hasn't faced?*

Intimacy shouldn't be a substitute for emotional presence. When it becomes that, it can leave the new partner feeling invisible, hurt, and torn. As Dr Susan J. Elliott [11] points out, unless the widower works through his grief, physical closeness alone cannot create the foundation for a healthy relationship.

I call this pattern the *Widower's Fire*, because it's something I've seen repeatedly in interviews and conversations with women navigating these relationships. It's not a term borrowed from experts;

it's a way of describing a very real, emotional phenomenon that often goes unnamed.

Through the following case studies, we will explore how this pattern can play out, its impact on the new partner, and the signs to watch for.

Case Study - Sophie and Mark

Sophie thought she was building a real relationship with Mark, a widower. But after a few months, she began to notice a pattern: their closeness only happened at night, in bed. Outside those hours, Mark was distant, emotionally absent, almost like she wasn't there at all.

Then, during a fleeting intimate moment, he accidentally called her by his late wife's name. Sophie froze. She had never felt so much like a placeholder, a stand-in, rather than someone truly loved. Mark apologised, but the damage lingered, Sophie felt cheap, used, and invisible.

She tried to talk to him about how this made her feel. He struggled to respond. Eventually, he admitted he wasn't really in love with her, he just valued the physical side of their relationship. For Sophie, the words hit like a hammer: she was nothing more than a warm body in his life, not a partner or equal. Unable to reconcile the imbalance, she ended things. And just three weeks later, she learned Mark had already moved on.

Case Study - Hannah and Richard

Hannah, a deeply religious woman, fell in love with Richard, a widower. She had always believed in saving intimacy for marriage. But Richard asked her to set aside her faith, assuring her he wanted a life together. He proposed, giving her a beautiful ring, one she later discovered had belonged to his late wife.

Feeling secure in his commitment, Hannah trusted him and stepped into intimacy. But after a few months, Richard confessed he never truly intended to remarry, doing so, he said, would dishonour his late wife. Heartbroken, Hannah struggled to process the betrayal. When she tried to talk about her pain, Richard ended the relationship abruptly, leaving her feeling cheap, used, and naive for compromising her values. The experience left her grappling with shame, regret, and a deep questioning of her own judgment and worth.

Recognising the Red Flags

Sophie and Hannah's stories unfold in very different ways, yet they reveal a shared truth about what happens when intimacy develops in the shadow of unresolved grief. Both women entered relationships with widowers who, on the surface, appeared ready to move forward, but beneath that, grief was still the quiet force shaping their emotional availability and their behaviour.

While Sophie's experience with Mark seemed loving at first, intimacy soon became the only way they connected. Outside of the bedroom, Mark was emotionally distant, unavailable, and even dismissive of her desire for closeness. When he accidentally called her by his late wife's name, Sophie felt like a substitute, a stand-in for someone she could never replace. Mark's withdrawal revealed that his affection was more about seeking comfort than in a genuine emotional partnership.

Hannah's experience followed a more overt pattern of emotional manipulation. Guided by her faith and values, she wanted to wait until marriage to share physical intimacy. Richard, her widowed partner, assured her of his lifelong commitment, even proposing marriage and giving her a ring, one that later turned out to have belonged to his late wife. When Richard eventually withdrew, saying that remarrying would "dishonour" his late wife, Hannah was left shattered. Her trust and beliefs had been compromised, and she felt humiliated and used, not only emotionally, but spiritually.

Even though Sophie's and Hannah's experiences were different, they both show the emotional toll of what I call the *Widower's Fire*, that intense surge of desire and closeness that can follow loss.

It might feel like love at first, but when it's fuelled by loneliness or grief that hasn't been faced, it can become a substitute for real emotional connection. As Dr Susan J. Elliott [11] explains, when a widower hasn't worked through his grief, intimacy can soothe pain without building true love. For the partner, this can feel confusing, leaving her unseen, unchosen, and emotionally unsafe.

Some common warning signs you might notice:

- **Touch without talk:** Physical closeness becomes the main (or only) connection, while conversations about feelings or needs are missing.
- **Living in the past:** He may idealise or focus on his past life with his late wife, making it hard to form real emotional bonds with you.

- **Dismissing your feelings:** Your concerns get labelled as "too sensitive" or "needy," or your feelings are invalidated.
- **Shadows of the past:** Repeated references to his late wife before, during or after intimacy are strong signals that grief still dominates.

Psychologists call this *instrumental intimacy* [14], when sexual closeness is a tool to cope rather than a shared expression of love. Author Abel Keogh [3], who experienced widowhood himself, notes that some men unconsciously seek comfort in new relationships to avoid their grief, creating imbalance and confusion for their partners. Research on "continuing bonds" [15] shows that a strong emotional connection to a deceased spouse can complicate new relationships, especially when it comes through intimacy. It may feel comforting in the short term, but it often leads to long-term emotional distance rather than real closeness.

The impact on the living partner can be heavy. Sophie and Hannah both felt invisible, unchosen, and stripped of self-worth. What looked like love was actually a reflection of the widower's unresolved attachment to the past, and for the partner, it could be emotionally and psychologically damaging, especially when intimacy becomes a cover for grief rather than a real bond.

Protecting Yourself: Setting Healthy Boundaries

Caring about a widower's grief is natural, but your emotional safety must come first. A few practices that help:

- Talk honestly about what intimacy means for both of you.
- Set boundaries around physical closeness, especially if it feels rushed, one-sided, or disconnected from emotional connection.
- Ask for reassurance that your relationship is grounded in the present, not just filling a void from the past.
- Take things slowly. Let emotional connection grow naturally.

- Pause and reflect if intimacy starts to feel confusing or draining.

As Dr Susan J. Elliott [8] notes, intimacy grounded in emotional honesty rather than avoidance protects both partners. True healing and connections require patience, openness, and respect for genuine love, not the rush to replace what was lost.

What to Remember

When love begins in the ashes of grief, it's easy to mistake warmth for healing. But if a widower's heart still belongs to the past, no amount of passion can build a future. Recognising these signs early can protect your heart from being burnt by the *Widowers Fire*.

Chapter 4 - Loving in the Shadows of a Memory

"It felt like she was in every conversation."

"His love story with her was always the main story. I was just the footnote."

"I thought I could handle it, until I realised, I couldn't even put my photo on the wall."

Being with a widower often means sharing space with the subtle, lingering presence of his late wife. The photos still hanging on the walls, an online profile left untouched, or the casual mentions of "what she would have done" or "what she would have liked", can become painful reminders that they are sharing space not just with a partner, but with a memory. For the unhealed widower, the connection to his late wife's memory can prevent him from fully living in the present, making it difficult to truly honour and cherish his new partner without feeling guilt.

When I began dating Bill, I never anticipated how central his previous relationship would become in ours. In the beginning, I felt deep compassion for his pain. Having experienced the loss of a significant other myself, I understood the ache of grief and admired his openness about it.

Early in our relationship, we spoke freely about birthdays and special occasions, how we would honour them, and what they meant to each of us. I shared my own story, shaped by past disappointments, small hopes, and a quiet wish to be seen and cherished. Bill spoke with tenderness and pride about how he had always made his late wife's special days memorable, how he loved celebrating her and making her feel special. At the time, I found this deeply touching, a reflection of loyalty and emotional depth. I believed I was with a man who truly knew how to love a woman. Only later did I begin to realise that much of his heart was still anchored in the past.

Over time, I started noticing a pattern. On anniversaries, holidays, and even in quiet moments, his grief would swell, and I felt like I was left on the shore while he was pulled somewhere I couldn't reach. Our conversations kept circling back to her, and I found myself making excuses for him, telling myself it was unfair to expect more from a man who had "been through so much." The truth was, I didn't know what to do. I'd never been in a relationship like this before. Even though we shared a home, a table, and a bed, I would at times feel completely alone.

When I eventually tried to express how I was feeling and the patterns I had noticed, Bill dismissed my conccrns. At one point, he even suggested that I was the one bringing his late wife up too often, as if my pain stemmed from jealousy rather than confusion. His deflections left me questioning my own perceptions, and in time, I began to question the relationship itself.

When our relationship ended, Bill confessed that he didn't know how to celebrate me, or our special dates, without feeling like he was dishonouring his late wife. I now understand that what hurt most wasn't simply the absence of celebration; it was realising and accepting that no matter how patient or loving I tried to be, his heart could not fully meet me.

Life with an unhealed widower can sometimes feel profoundly lonely, even when you share the same space. Despite moments of closeness, there can be an underlying sense that part of your partner's heart still belongs to another time. Reminders of a past love can create invisible barriers, making it difficult to experience true emotional intimacy, not just in relationships with widowers, but in any partnership.

Many ex-partners of unhealed widowers described the moments when they felt like outsiders in their own relationships, quietly competing with memories they could never replace. I experienced this too; unprocessed grief kept Bill emotionally distant and unavailable often throughout the year. There were times I struggled not to take his distance personally. I found it difficult to explain what I was feeling or why.

The powerful presence of a late wife's memory can feel so vivid and 'in the now' that it overshadows the present relationship. An unhealed widower's expressions of grief, along with preserved routines, can make the new partner feel like she is competing for heart space with someone who is no longer alive. Psychotherapist Megan Devine [7], in her book "It's *OK That You're Not OK*", explains how grief reshapes relationships, that *"Grief creates a world where someone can be physically present yet emotionally elsewhere."* Megan's words reflect an everyday reality for many partners of unhealed widowers, who often feel as though the man they love is still partly living in another time and place.

To those on the outside, it may seem loving or even admirable when a widower keeps his late wife's memory close. Yet for his new partner, it can bring an ache few understand, a feeling of being present but unseen, as if she is living in the shadows of a ghost.

Case Study - Mel and Barry

Mel had been with Barry for just over two years when she began to notice a quiet uneasy feeling growing within. Barry, a widower, had photos of his late wife everywhere, on his phone, laptop, and carefully organised in albums. At first, Mel tried to look at the pictures as a way for Barry to remember someone he had loved. She wanted to respect that, even if it sometimes made her feel a little off balance.

As their relationship developed, Mel found it increasingly difficult to ignore the sense of being surrounded by another woman's memory. She had never been in a relationship where grief was such a visible presence. Watching Barry's emotional responses as he revisited old photographs left her uncertain about where she fit in his life and heart.

Early in the relationship, Mel tried to raise her concerns gently, but when she did, Barry grew emotional, saying she could never understand the depth of his loss. After this conversation, Mel felt she could no longer speak openly about her feelings without causing him further pain. She also found it difficult when Barry continued to call his late wife 'his wife', as it reinforced the sense that she was sharing her partner's affection with someone no longer alive.

One of the most challenging aspects for Mel was the shrine Barry had created for his late wife, a large display on the living room coffee table filled with candles, photos, personal mementos, and an urn. The shrine dominated the shared space, and Mel often hesitated to use the table for everyday things, fearing it might appear disrespectful. She initially assumed that, as their relationship deepened, the shrine might naturally become smaller or be moved to a less central place in the home. However, Barry firmly stated that it would remain exactly as it was.

Mel was aware that the main bedroom and bathroom remained largely untouched. His late wife's clothing still hung in the wardrobe, and some of her perfumes and toiletries remained on the shelves. These constant reminders reinforced the feeling that Mel was living alongside a preserved past rather than building a new life together.

Over time, a pattern emerged. Barry became withdrawn every Saturday, the day his late wife had passed away. When combined with other significant dates such as anniversaries and birthdays, Mel realised that Barry was emotionally unavailable for a large portion of the year.

Feeling isolated and overshadowed by a woman she had never met, Mel sought advice from friends. Their responses tended to focus on Barry's loss, "It must be hard to lose someone you love", rather than acknowledging her own emotional experience. This lack of understanding left Mel feeling even more alone.

Eventually, feeling heartbroken, Mel decided to end the relationship. She had realised that Barry was still deeply connected to his late wife's memory and was not yet emotionally ready to create space for her.

Case Study - Susan and Sam

Susan, an accomplished businesswoman and award-winning restaurateur, met Sam through mutual friends. They quickly discovered a shared love of food, wine, and conversation, an effortless connection that gave Susan hope for something meaningful.

Early in their relationship, Susan noticed that Sam spoke often and fondly of his late wife, Molly. Though it sometimes made her uncomfortable, Susan cared deeply for Sam and wanted to know all parts of his story, even those that hurt to hear. She told herself that listening to his memories was part of truly knowing him, and she gently pushed aside her own feelings of unease.

But over time, Susan realised that every topic seemed to circle back to Molly. Whether they were discussing weekend plans, a new recipe, or a holiday destination, Sam would inevitably compare it to something he and Molly had shared or to Molly's talents and preferences.

One day, Susan's restaurant received a prestigious regional award for excellence, recognising two of its signature dishes: the house-made lasagne crafted with locally raised beef, and the fresh fettuccine marinara with shellfish sourced from nearby waters. Overjoyed, Susan invited Sam to the restaurant to celebrate. She arranged for the head chef to personally serve them the award-winning dishes, hoping to share her pride and excitement.

When the food arrived, Susan eagerly watched Sam taste the lasagne, then the fettuccine. Smiling, she asked, "What do you think?"

Sam took another bite and casually replied, *"It's not bad, but not as good as Molly's. She really knew how to cook Italian food; everyone in the family raved about it. If she were still alive, you could've hired her to replace your head chef."*

The words landed like a stone in Susan's chest. Shocked and hurt, she quietly told Sam about the award, but the moment felt ruined. Overwhelmed, she excused herself and stepped into the back of the restaurant, fighting back tears.

When she returned to the table, Sam had pulled up photos of Molly's cooking on his phone and excitedly showed them to Susan. Susan was unsure what to say, so she just politely nodded along. Then the head chef approached the table, keen to hear Sam's thoughts. Instead of complimenting the chef's food, Sam started praising Molly's cooking. The chef looked at Susan, puzzled, who blushed with embarrassment. In that moment, it felt almost as if she were an outsider in her own restaurant.

The chef quietly returned to the kitchen. Susan felt humiliated, invisible, and deeply sad that Sam hadn't acknowledged the award or offered genuine praise for the food she and her team had worked so hard to perfect.

Susan's appetite vanished. Sam, seemingly unaware, continued reminiscing about Molly's recipes and family meals. At the end of the evening, he asked if

Susan wanted to go back to his house for a few drinks. She politely declined.

Driving home, Susan held her emotions until she walked through her front door and then broke down in tears. She didn't just feel overshadowed by Molly; she felt completely unseen, as though there was no space for her achievements, her feelings, or even her presence in Sam's heart.

Recognising the Red Flags

The experiences of Mel with Barry and Susan with Sam reveal the subtle yet painful ways unresolved grief can affect new relationships. Both women entered their relationships with empathy and patience, understanding that love after loss carries complexity. Yet, despite their compassion, they each came to recognise patterns that suggested their partners were not emotionally ready to build a shared future.

In Barry's case, grief was made visible through his environment, the preserved belongings, the shrine, and the unchanged spaces. His home was a physical extension of his inner world: filled with symbols of attachment that had not transitioned from mourning to memory. Grief expert James Worden explains in his *Tasks of Mourning* model, one essential aspect of adapting to loss is the ability to "emotionally relocate" the deceased and reinvest in life [38]. When this task is incomplete, the bereaved may continue to relate to their loved one as though they are still central in daily life. Barry's insistence that nothing be altered and his emotional withdrawal on significant dates suggested that his grief remained active rather than integrated. For Mel, this meant that love could never fully take hold in the present; she was living beside his past rather than within his present.

In Susan's story, grief showed itself less through things and more through words. Sam kept comparing her to his late wife, Molly, which is a kind of *'continuing bond'*, which researchers describe as the way someone stays connected to a person who has died [17]. That bond can be healthy, even comforting, but it becomes a problem when the deceased turns it into an unspoken standard that new partners are measured against.

For Susan, almost every conversation seemed to come back to Molly. She felt invisible and unvalued. The moment it hit hardest was when Sam compared her award-winning dishes to Molly's cooking. His admiration, his affection, stayed locked on someone who was gone, while the woman in front of him, alive, present, and giving her all, went unnoticed.

In these relationships, the late wife's presence lingered in conversation, ritual, and space, creating an emotional triangle where the new partner was left feeling secondary. The widower's loyalty to his late wife, though often unconscious, created barriers to intimacy and mutual recognition.

These stories show some common red flags that a widower's grief might still be unresolved:

- **Physical reminders everywhere:** Shrines, untouched belongings, or rooms preserved exactly as they were can signal that the deceased still occupies the emotional centre of the home.

- **Constant comparisons:** When he keeps referring back to the late spouse or their qualities, it puts the new partner in a position of emotional competition she can never win.

- **Emotional absence on key dates:** Anniversaries, birthdays, and holidays can leave the living partner feeling invisible when rituals of remembrance overshadow the new relationship.

- **Guilt-driven interactions:** If expressing your discomfort triggers defensiveness or emotional withdrawal from him, then the relationship might be based on guilt rather than connection.

Experts say these patterns usually mean the widower's grief hasn't fully moved from intense mourning to a more settled, integrated stage. Psychologists note that healthy grieving involves a back-and-forth, facing the loss at times, and engaging with life at others [5]. When too much focus stays on the past, there's very little room left for emotional availability or for forming a real connection in the present.

For women like Mel and Susan, that imbalance can feel suffocating. They weren't competing with another person; they were competing with a memory that could never respond, change, or love them back. Unhealed grief can turn remembrance into a barrier, keeping new love in the shadow of the past.

Honouring a late spouse and embracing a new relationship aren't mutually exclusive, but it takes conscious effort, honesty, and willingness to make space for both. As grief expert Kenneth Doka notes, *"grief does not end, but it must evolve"* [44]. When a widower can't evolve, he risks keeping both himself and his partner trapped in the past.

Ultimately, love after loss requires emotional integration, carrying the memory forward without letting it define the present. Without that integration, even the most caring partner can end up not beside the man she loves, but living among his ghosts.

What to Remember

When a widower's past love dominates through memories, belongings, or comparisons, it can overshadow his current relationship, leaving his new partner feeling invisible and constantly measured against someone she can never replace. Spotting these red flags early helps determine if he's ready to fully embrace the present. True love after loss requires balancing remembrance with living in the now.

Chapter 5 - Living in a Three-Way Relationship.

"Some days, it feels like she's still the love of his life, and I'm just the woman he comes home to."

"I wanted to respect his grief, but I didn't want to build my future standing in someone else's shadow."

"The hardest part isn't the photos or anniversaries; it's feeling that his happiest memories are with her, not me."

In this chapter, we examine the emotional complexity that arises when a widower, still grieving and in love with his late wife, enters a new relationship. This dynamic can be described as a "three-way relationship", and it can create discomfort, tension, and confusion for everyone involved. We'll explore what it means for a widower to carry his late wife's affection and memories while loving someone new, and how the new partner may feel inadequate, compare themselves, or feel the need for acceptance.

In my view, three-way relationships are not for the faint-hearted. From conversations with many women in this situation, it's clear that unhealed widowers often prioritise their own emotional needs, keeping strong ties to their late wife while expecting their new partner to adapt to a reality unlike any other relationship. This can mean living in, or regularly visiting, a home where it feels as though his late wife could walk back in at any moment, her belongings and memories scattered throughout the house.

Some unhealed widowers may hope or even expect their new partner to accept the ongoing presence of their late wife, often without realising how emotionally demanding this can be. This can create a tension between the past and the present, leaving the new partner feeling overlooked, conflicted, or uncertain of her place in the relationship. The memory of Bill's late wife turned up a lot in our relationship, from his frequent memories of their life together to the physical memorials he maintained to the recurring emotional withdrawal around anniversaries. Gradually, I experienced a growing sense of displacement, as though I was standing in a space that never truly felt like mine.

Drawing on professional insights and real-life experiences, this chapter highlights the emotional strain, confusion, and challenges that arise when a widower's grief remains unresolved. Through case studies and expert commentary, readers will see how these dynamics can affect intimacy, communication, and the sense of security in the relationship. The goal is to underscore that being in a "three-way" emotional dynamic is deeply complex and not for everyone, and to help readers recognise the realities of loving someone whose heart is partly still with the past.

Case Study - Mindy and Derick

Mindy had been dating Derick, a widower, for several months. They spent most of their time together at her home. She deeply loved Derick and envisioned a long, happy future together. Everything felt right until the night she stayed over at Derick's house for the first time. As they went to bed, Mindy was struck by the room's deeply preserved memory of Derick's late wife: clothes draped over a chair, wedding photos on the walls, and a glamorous portrait above the bed. Derick's late wife's wedding dress still hung in the wardrobe, and her ashes and wedding ring rested on his bedside table.

That night, Mindy felt overwhelmed and suddenly out of place. What began as intimacy turned into emotional distance; she wanted to cry and go home rather than stay in a space that felt sacred to another woman. The next morning, Mindy watched Derick kiss his late wife's photo and whisper, "Good morning, beautiful," before turning to greet her. This moment left Mindy feeling as though she were intruding on a marriage that hadn't truly ended, leading to guilt, confusion, and the unsettling sense of being "the other woman."

Later that day, Mindy asked Derick if he was ready to be in a new relationship, as she felt that he was still actively in love with his late wife. Mindy felt as if her relationship with Derick was a threesome, with the third person invisible. Mindy wondered if she was, in fact, the invisible one, and she really struggled to feel safe to love a man who wanted her to acknowledge, love, and respect his late wife, a person that she had never met. She tried to discuss her thoughts with Derick, but he became defensive and accused Mindy of trying to erase his late wife's memory. Mindy refused to stay at Derick's house as it made her feel very uncomfortable. Derick refused to make any changes to his life out of respect for his late wife and suggested that Mindy was the one with the problem. Mindy ended the relationship. Derrick started a new relationship four weeks later.

Case Study - Jeanette and Lindsay

Jeanette had been dating Lindsay, a widower, for ten months when she was invited to his house for dinner. Lindsay often brought his late wife into conversations, something Jeanette found difficult but couldn't express easily. She sometimes felt guilty, wondering if she was being unreasonable or jealous of a woman who had passed away.

When Jeanette finally shared her discomfort, Lindsay reacted defensively. He insisted his late wife was the love of his life, and no one could replace her. Lindsay told Jeanette she should feel honoured to sit where his late wife once did and said that to be with him, she needed to understand the love he has for his late wife. Jeanette felt hurt and used, as if her presence served to fill the space rather than build a new relationship.

When Jeanette asked if Lindsay spoke about his ex-girlfriend this way to his late wife, Lindsay replied that it was different because his ex was still alive, and that talking about her wouldn't have been appropriate. He explained that losing the love of your life changes everything, and that Jeanette needed to accept this if they were to stay together.

Feeling increasingly like "the other woman," Jeanette chose to end the relationship. Lindsay later told others that Jeanette was jealous of a dead woman, which further deepened Jeanette's sadness.

Recognising the Red Flags

The experiences of Mindy with Derick and Jeanette with Lindsay reveal patterns that often signal challenges in relationships with unhealed widowers. Mindy's discomfort arose from the physical presence of Derick's late wife: clothes draped over chairs, wedding photos on the walls, a shrine, ashes and personal mementos by the bed. Being in this space made her feel like an intruder in a life still devoted to someone else, leaving her guilt-ridden, anxious, and emotionally sidelined. When she attempted to discuss her feelings, Derick became defensive, suggesting she was trying to erase his late wife's memory, which ultimately led Mindy to end the relationship.

Jeanette's struggle was more emotional than physical. Lindsay insisted that to love him, she must also love and honour his late wife. Almost every conversation circled back to his late wife, often framing Jeanette's role as one of acceptance rather than partnership. When she expressed her discomfort, Lindsay became defensive, leaving Jeanette feeling invisible, undervalued, and emotionally overshadowed. She eventually chose to leave the relationship, recognising that she could not share a life where someone else's memory dominated the present.

These stories show how unresolved grief can quietly take over a widower's emotional world, potentially leaving his new partner feeling sidelined. As Dr Susan J. Elliott [11] explains, when grief is tangled up with new love, the partner can start to feel like a placeholder instead of someone fully seen and valued. Grief expert David Kessler [2] puts it simply: *"The goal isn't to forget, but to remember with more love than pain."* The trick, and the challenge, is carrying the memory forward without letting it crowd out the present.

Pauline Boss [12] explains that when the deceased remains central in family life, "boundary confusion" and relational ambiguity often occur, leaving a new partner competing with someone who is no longer alive. Recognising these patterns early helps new partners understand whether a widower is emotionally ready to create space for a shared present. Without conscious effort, grief can transform remembrance into an invisible barrier, preventing the relationship from developing fully and leaving the new partner living under the shadow of a memory.

Practical Strategies to Keep the Balance:

- **Open discussion:** Share your feelings honestly, without blaming your partner for grieving, but stand firm in your convictions. Use "I feel" statements to express discomfort and distress.

- **Set gentle boundaries:** It's fair to you and the health of your relationship to ask for private spaces in the home or to limit conversations about his late wife and to fully exclude his late wife's memory during intimate moments.

- **Create new traditions:** talk about the importance of building traditions unique to your relationship, such as lunch dates, travel destinations unique to you both, or shared hobbies that are not linked to his past. It's important to establish your identity as a couple in love.

- **Acknowledge past anniversaries mindfully:** Encourage your partner to honour meaningful dates in a way that finds ways for you to stay emotionally connected rather than excluded.

When grief remains unresolved and boundaries are blurred, the effect on a new partner can be profound, a topic we will explore in the next chapter.

What to Remember

A widower's unresolved grief can overshadow a new relationship, leaving the partner feeling unseen and measured against the past. Recognising these patterns early helps determine if a shared future is possible.

Chapter 6 - When Grief Shadows Love

"Every big step forward, he'd pull back."

"His guilt was stronger than his hope."

"I kept thinking time would fix it, but time alone changed nothing."

Grief is deeply personal, and for widowers, it can show up in ways that are complicated and sometimes confusing for a new partner. Unresolved grief can raise difficult questions and cast a long shadow over new love.

By the time women begin questioning a widower's readiness, many describe the same feeling, being quietly forced to compete with a past that has not yet been laid to rest. It's less about the obvious signs, which have already been explored, and more about the emotional atmosphere. Plans for the future may feel vague or postponed, affection may feel inconsistent, and conversations about commitment are often avoided or uncomfortable.

Noticing these dynamics isn't about assigning fault. It's about understanding whether he is genuinely able to show up in the present, honour the woman beside him, and build something based on shared commitment, respect, and emotional availability.

Discussions with other women whose relationships with widowers ended reveal a common theme: many men don't realise they are not yet ready to love again. Often, they fail to see how ongoing grief and an inability to make emotional space can hinder a new relationship.

Some unhealed widowers rush into relationships to escape loneliness or avoid their pain. This dynamic, which I call the *Widower's Fire,* can feel passionate and consuming at first, but it's often more about filling emptiness than genuinely moving forward. In my own experience, it wasn't until my relationship with Bill ended that I understood he had been seeking a way to soothe his grief, not to build a shared future with me. Unhealed grief can profoundly affect new relationships, unintentionally causing emotional harm, a reality that many women, myself included, only recognise too late.

Case Study -Tracy and Tom

Tom began dating Tracy six months after his late wife passed, meeting her through an online dating site. He told Tracy he was ready to love again, and for the first year, their relationship was filled with joy, passion, and the sense that Tracy had found her soulmate. She truly believed Tom was the man she wanted to spend her life with.

The challenges emerged when Tracy gently tried to discuss their future. She hoped for marriage, but Tom was firm; he could not marry again after losing the love of his life. Tracy felt rejected and heartbroken, emotions that began to strain their once-happy relationship.

Tom explained that he felt torn, unable to bridge the gap between his grief and Tracy's expectations. He suggested that Tracy's concerns were a sign of her being "too sensitive," leaving her feeling invisible and questioning her worth. Tom's refusal to understand Tracy's point of view left her feeling emotionally isolated.

His commitment to preserving the memory of his late wife became a barrier to intimacy. Over time, Tom clung ever more tightly to the past, weighed down by fear and guilt, while Tracy became increasingly drained and unfulfilled. Eventually, she recognised that Tom's love was for the memory of his late wife, and that she was, in effect, a temporary distraction from his grief. The relationship ultimately ended.

Case Study – Sophia and Mark

Mark began dating Sophia two years after the death of his girlfriend. As the third anniversary of her passing approached, he started drinking heavily to numb his grief. Sophia noticed that his drinking and emotional withdrawal coincided with anniversary dates and other significant occasions he had once shared with his late girlfriend. During these times, he often cut off communication entirely for weeks, leaving Sophia feeling ghosted, heartbroken, and unseen.

When Sophia tried to share her feelings, Mark explained that he was experiencing normal stages of grief and missed his late girlfriend, insisting that Sophia still had a place in his life. She expressed how much it hurt to be shut out for weeks, but Mark said he couldn't control his reactions to loss.

Over time, Sophia realised that Mark was still deeply grieving and not ready to fully engage in a new relationship. What she initially thought was love left her feeling used, second-best, and invisible. Recognising the emotional imbalance, Sophia ended the relationship and encouraged Mark to focus on his own healing before inviting another partner into his life.

Case Study – Melinda and David

When Melinda met David online, their connection felt immediate and genuine. They shared so much in common: golf, cycling, hiking, and both were single parents to children of similar ages. David's late wife had passed away just ten months earlier, and although Melinda had initial reservations about the timing, he appeared warm, kind, and said that he was ready to open his heart again.

For the first few months, their relationship unfolded naturally and felt full of promise. They spent weekends outdoors, enjoying simple adventures together, and often talked about one day blending their families. Melinda believed she had finally met someone she could build a life with. But as time went on, small cracks began to appear, ones that had less to do with their connection and more to do with the lingering influence of David's past and his ties to his late wife's family.

Melinda first met David's late wife's family at his eldest daughter's birthday party, just a few months into their relationship. She had lovingly prepared most of the food and even baked the cake, hoping to make the day special for David and his children. But the family's reception was distant and uneasy. Later, they expressed to David that they believed he had moved on too soon and that Melinda was trying to take the place of their beloved. From that moment, things changed. They began hosting family-only barbecues, dinners, and memorial events, often in honour of David's late wife, where Melinda was deliberately excluded. Their quiet disapproval became a constant presence in the background of the relationship.

Despite this, David continued to maintain close ties with his late wife's family. Melinda understood that connection was important to him, but the stronger their influence became, the more distant he grew. He began cancelling plans and avoiding conversations about their future. Melinda felt increasingly uncertain about her place in his life, like a visitor standing outside a family circle she could never enter.

The breaking point came when David went on a two-week holiday with his children and his late wife's family to his late wife's favourite destination, a trip to celebrate what would have been his late wife's birthday. When he returned, he called Melinda and said he wanted to "take a break" from their relationship, explaining that his children and family needed him and that he wanted to focus on spending more time with them.

Melinda was devastated. She felt blindsided and used, left wondering whether David had ever truly been ready, or if she had merely filled a space left empty by grief and guilt.

Recognising the Red Flags

Across these stories, a common thread emerges: love entered before grief had a chance to heal. While each relationship looked promising at first, the undercurrent of unresolved loss created emotional distance, confusion, and pain for the women involved.

In Tracy's case, Tom's loyalty to his late wife became an invisible wall between them. Though he cared deeply for Tracy, his declaration that he could never remarry because he had already lost "the love of his life" revealed a heart still bound to the past. His grief, unacknowledged and unprocessed, left Tracy feeling like a placeholder rather than a partner.

For Sophia, the red flag appeared in patterns of emotional withdrawal. Mark's recurring grief around anniversaries and his inability to remain emotionally present left her feeling abandoned. Instead of turning toward her for support, he turned inward and numbed his pain. Grief expert Dr Kenneth Doka [44] explains that when someone carries disenfranchised grief, grief that isn't openly acknowledged or supported, it can creep into new relationships in ways that make emotional closeness and honest communication really difficult.

Melinda's story showed a different kind of red flag: pressure from the late wife's family and David's struggle to set healthy boundaries. His loyalty to them made sense, but it got in the way of emotional independence and the chance to build a future together. His fear of upsetting the past ultimately cost him the relationship he had in front of him.

The emotional boundaries were blurred, and the memory of the late wife stays central, making it hard for the living partner to connect fully. As mentioned earlier, Psychologist Pauline Boss [12] calls this *ambiguous loss*.

Each of these stories demonstrates that unresolved grief does not always appear as sadness; it can look like avoidance, guilt, loyalty conflicts, or a reluctance to invest in the future fully. These behaviours often signal that a widower is not emotionally available, no matter how sincere his intentions may seem.

Grief professionals emphasise that healthy mourning involves four key tasks: accepting the reality of the loss, processing the pain, adjusting to life without the deceased, and finding a way to carry their memory forward [4]. When one or more of these tasks remain incomplete, the widower may unconsciously keep one foot in the past, preventing emotional intimacy with a new partner.

Recognising the red flags early can help women decide if a widower is genuinely ready for a relationship or still healing. When grief is unresolved, love becomes entwined with loss. As David Kessler reminds us, *"The goal isn't to forget, but to remember with more love than pain."* [2]. Until that balance is found, relationships can get stuck in a cycle, moments of closeness followed by emotional distance, leaving unintentional hurt in their wake.

These case studies remind us that recognising emotional readiness is essential. It takes honesty and courage for both partners to acknowledge when grief still occupies too much space in the relationship. Love after loss is possible, but only when the past is respected without being allowed to rule the present.

What To Remember

Healing personal grief doesn't mean that the past is forgotten. It means making space for the present and embracing life.

Dear Me

I wanted to be the one to bring you back to life. At first, your devotion felt moving, proof of the kind of partner you could be: loyal, loving, committed.

I thought love could fix what grief had left behind. I stood quietly beside your past, believing that waiting made me noble. I silenced my own hurt because I thought that was what compassion looked like. But love shouldn't feel like fading away. I was allowed to want more than just a spot beside a ghost. I should have been able to speak about my needs without guilt. I needed to be loved in the present, not just tolerated in someone else's unfinished story.

One day, I will realise that wanting to be fully chosen isn't selfish. When that day comes, I won't be standing in the shadows anymore. I will be living my own life, whole, visible, and finally free.

I forgive myself for feeling sad and lonely, for giving so many years to someone who never truly loved me. I forgive myself for feeling like I never quite belonged.

And most of all, I forgive myself for not seeing the red flags before I was deeply hurt.

Part 2- In Memory of Someone I Didn't Know

During my time with Bill, one truth gradually became impossible to ignore: he struggled to remain emotionally present in our relationship, especially around the anniversaries he had shared with his late wife. In the first year, I didn't fully understand what was happening. I asked if he was okay, but he always insisted he was fine, offering no real explanation.

By the second year, I noticed a pattern. He would grow quiet and withdrawn for weeks before and after those significant dates. When I gently raised my concerns, he dismissed them, saying only that he wasn't feeling well or had been feeling tired. Wanting to be supportive, I gave him the benefit of the doubt again and again.

By our third year together, I finally found the courage to name what I was seeing and how I felt. Instead of opening up, Bill accused me of being unsupportive and, to my shock, discussed his frustrations with my adult children behind my back, stating that I wouldn't let him talk about his late wife and that I was being insensitive. I turned my thoughts inward, questioning my compassion and character. *"Am I jealous of a dead woman?"* I'd ask myself. *"Am I being unkind?"* Despite searching, I found little guidance or literature that spoke to what I was living through.

I had never been in a relationship with a widower before, and while I genuinely wanted to support Bill, his recurring withdrawal left me feeling sad, unseen, and emotionally abandoned. Trying to make sense of my confusion, I joined an online support group for women dating widowers, something I stumbled upon by chance. There, I found story after story that echoed my own: partners who pulled away around anniversaries, shut down emotionally, or seemed to slip back into old memories just as their new relationship began to deepen.

When our relationship ended after five years, I was heartbroken. Bill, who once was loving and kind, had become distant and critical. I blamed myself for ignoring the warning signs, for investing years in someone who couldn't meet me halfway.

Looking back, I see things more clearly now. Grief deserves compassion but love also deserves mutuality. A living partner should never be asked to exist in the shadows of the past. Recognising that truth isn't unkind, it's essential.

Part Two of this book explores the emotional complexities that often arise when loving a widower who has not yet healed from his loss. Drawing from both my own experiences and the insights of many other women, this section aims to bring awareness to the subtle, often hidden challenges that can quietly shape these relationships.

We'll look closely at why some widowers emotionally shut down around anniversary dates once shared with their late wife, and why they may feel compelled to keep a "shrine" or hold tightly to her belongings. We'll explore how social media can reopen wounds or create confusion, and why certain widowers continue to speak about their late wife in the present tense, as though she still occupies a space beside them.

Understanding these patterns isn't about judgment; it's about clarity. By recognising the emotional and behavioural signs of unresolved grief, we can better protect our own wellbeing while fostering compassion grounded in reality, not illusion.

Chapter 7 – Anniversaries

"I could feel my anxiety build as the anniversary of his late wife's death approached".

"He shut down before and after important dates he shared with his late wife".

"He didn't acknowledge our first anniversary, he forgot the date, yet I know all the old anniversary dates he shared with her".

Widowers often feel fresh waves of grief, guilt, or emotional strain around specific dates attached to their past relationship. These days can hit hard, stirring up loss, regret, or unresolved guilt and reminding them just how deep their attachment was. Experts note that when a widower hasn't fully processed his grief, these anniversaries can lead to emotional withdrawal, irritability, or sudden distance. It's rarely intentional, but it can leave the new partner feeling pushed aside or invisible just when closeness is needed most.

Through the online support group and many heartfelt conversations with women who have loved widowers, I discovered that this pattern is strikingly common. Many unhealed widowers feel compelled to publicly honour the anniversary dates they once shared with their late wife. While this often stems from loyalty and love, it can create painful emotional imbalance, especially when the new partner is excluded from his life during those times. She may find herself needing reassurance yet receiving silence instead.

This tension between honouring the past and nurturing the present can quietly erode intimacy and trust. Some widowers participate in memorial events or host remembrance gatherings that, while meaningful to them, can unintentionally deepen emotional conflict if these rituals overshadow their current relationship.

Grief experts emphasise that true healing and connection come through open conversation and thoughtful boundaries. Discussing how anniversaries will be marked and creating new traditions that honour the past while prioritising the present can help the new partner to feel included, seen, and valued in the relationship.

Conversations with women who have loved widowers reveal a striking pattern: relationships often unravel, or even end, around key anniversaries and memorial dates. Unhealed grief can quietly set the emotional tempo of a partnership, quietly dictating closeness, distance, and tension, unless both partners actively confront it together. The following case studies illustrate how these dynamics play out in real relationships, highlighting the challenges and emotional impact on the new partner.

Case Study - Wendy and Alan

Wendy has been dating Alan for six years, whose late wife passed away ten years ago. Each year around the anniversary of his late wife's death, Alan emotionally and mentally shuts down, leaving Wendy feeling shut out and invisible. Alan insists on organising memorial events in honour of his late wife and expects Wendy to attend and support him. Despite Wendy's repeated attempts to express how sidelined she feels during these periods, Alan continues to acknowledge his late wife's birthday, date of death and wedding anniversary with memorial-style events.

Wendy noticed that, in total, Alan spends nearly two months each year focused on his late wife, during which he neglects Wendy's emotional and intimate needs. This makes Wendy question whether her relationship with Alan is as meaningful to him as his marriage to his late wife was.

Alan and his late wife didn't have children, so his ongoing need to hold yearly memorial events has become increasingly confusing and painful for Wendy. She has sought therapy to cope emotionally, yet Alan dismisses her concerns as oversensitivity and feels she should be more understanding. Wendy now struggles with feeling like she is living permanently in the shadow of a ghost, questioning her place in Alan's life and the future of their relationship.

Case Study - James and Kelly

James and Kelly have been married for eleven years and have three children together. James also has two adult children (aged 20 and 22) from his late wife. Each year, James feels compelled to honour the anniversary of his late wife's passing, largely for the sake of his older children. Despite Kelly being in their lives as a mother figure for twelve years, longer than their late mother was, James's adult children insist on continuing graveside rituals, expecting Kelly and her younger children to attend out of respect.

As their younger children have grown, they have expressed discomfort with these memorials. They feel uneasy seeing their older siblings and father become distant and emotional around these dates. This has led them to ask Kelly if they can stay home instead of attending. When Kelly tried to discuss this with James, he raised it with his adult children, who accused Kelly of putting ideas into the younger children's heads and dismissed their feelings.

Kelly never wanted to attend these memorials but did so out of love and respect, only to find herself feeling conflicted. Kelly feels caught between supporting her husband, honouring her late husband's memory, and protecting her own children from distress. The late wife's extended family also pressured Kelly and the younger children to attend, insisting it was important to honour their father's grief. Kelly felt torn between trying to balance everyone's needs while protecting her own family's emotional well-being.

Case Study: Emily and Daniel

Emily and Daniel had been dating for just under a year. Daniel's late wife had passed away three years earlier, and their wedding anniversary remained a particularly emotional time for him. Early in their relationship, Emily realised that their dating anniversary fell almost exactly on Daniel's wedding anniversary with his late wife. Daniel said this period was especially difficult, and, recognising the emotional strain it caused, he suggested they move their anniversary date by a month. After discussing it with her therapist, Emily agreed. Daniel was relieved by the change, but he made it clear that he couldn't fully focus on their anniversary until the emotionally heavy week had passed.

The week leading up to Daniel's late wife's anniversary proved exceptionally challenging. He frequently expressed uncertainty about how he would feel over the weekend and asked Emily if they could see each other, which she agreed to, even though the uncertainty left her feeling anxious and unsettled. During this time, he often spoke of his late wife, recalling past conversations and praising her, which left Emily feeling overshadowed and emotionally exhausted. She struggled with the conflict between wanting to support him and feeling invisible in the shadow of his grief.

Even when they managed to have a pleasant lunch together midweek, Emily noticed how quickly Daniel's sadness returned. Emily, who prides herself on caring for her partner and helping them feel supported, felt powerless in the face of his waves of grief. Each evening, his withdrawal and depression left her questioning whether anything she did could make a difference. She found herself wrestling with thoughts like, *"Don't I help you at all? Aren't you grateful for me?"*, though she never voiced these questions, knowing they wouldn't be helpful. The emotional tension made conversations awkward, and Emily began going to bed feeling drained and tearful.

One week before Daniel's wedding anniversary with his late wife, and just one day after what would have been their original dating anniversary, Daniel ended the relationship. Emily was left heartbroken, aware that no matter how attentive or loving she was, she could not take away the grief he carried. She had been caught in the difficult position of wanting to support him fully while simultaneously protecting her own emotional well-being, only to realise that his unresolved grief had dominated their relationship.

Case Study – Laura and Matthew

Laura and Matthew had been together for four years. Deeply in love, Laura had sold her assets and moved in with him, believing they were building a future together. For the first few years, their relationship felt close and supportive, but over time, Laura began noticing troubling patterns. On all the anniversary dates Matthew had shared with his late wife, he became quiet, sullen, and withdrawn. When she asked him about it, he insisted he was fine and that she was "stressing over nothing."

Confused and seeking clarity, Laura sought support from friends. Still, they struggled to understand the hidden complexities of being in a relationship with a widower and encouraged her to be more understanding and supportive of his grief. Instead of feeling validated, Laura felt as though she was the one creating distance in the relationship, leaving her even more bewildered and emotionally drained.

The truth finally came when Matthew admitted that he had not truly loved Laura for some time. Although he had enjoyed her companionship, support, and presence, he was no longer able to sustain a committed, loving relationship. Devastatingly, he asked if they could continue seeing each other as "friends with benefits." Laura, who had been deeply in love with him, was left heartbroken, extremely sad, and feeling mentally drained. She felt as if everything good in their relationship had been an illusion, and her world had turned completely upside down.

Making things even harder, Matthew ended the relationship just two weeks before the anniversary of his wedding to his late wife. For Laura, it reinforced the painful sense that she had been competing with a past that she could never win. She had sold her own assets to move in with him, and now she felt deeply betrayed, as if her love, trust, and presence had been taken for granted rather than truly valued.

This experience left Laura reeling, financially exhausted, emotionally shattered, and questioning how she had been so deeply invested in someone who had been unable to return her love fully.

Recognising the Red Flags

Looking across the stories of Wendy, James, Emily, and Laura, some clear patterns start to emerge. Recognising these red flags can help partners understand what it's really like to be in a relationship with an unhealed widower and make choices that protect their own well-being. Every relationship is different, of course, but common themes recur, leaving the new partner feeling sidelined, invisible, or emotionally torn.

Anniversaries and memorial triggers appear repeatedly. Wendy noticed that Alan shut down emotionally around the anniversary of his late wife's death, organising memorial-style events that left her feeling sidelined for nearly two months each year. Similarly, Emily found herself caught in the shadow of Daniel's grief, even after moving their dating anniversary to reduce emotional tension. Daniel frequently swung between withdrawal and nostalgia, leaving Emily drained and questioning whether her support made any difference. Laura experienced similar patterns with Matthew, who grew quiet and sullen on all the anniversary dates he had shared with his late wife, dismissing her concerns and leaving her feeling responsible for the distance in the relationship. These triggers can leave partners feeling powerless, uncertain, and emotionally exhausted, highlighting how unresolved grief can overshadow the present relationship [8][20].

Family and social pressures can make these situations even trickier. James felt he had to honour his late wife for his adult children's sake. At the same time, Kelly, who had been a central figure in their lives for over ten years, was stuck trying to support her husband, manage his children's expectations, and protect her own younger kids. Stories like this show how divided loyalties and outside pressure can add emotional strain, leaving the current partner feeling sidelined and torn [4].

Another common theme is emotional neglect or feeling unheard. Wendy's attempts to share her feelings were brushed off as oversensitivity. Emily's concerns about feeling invisible were mostly ignored. Laura was even told by friends to be more supportive of Matthew's grief, which left her feeling more confused and drained.

Across these experiences, partners often carry guilt, wondering if they're the problem or if they're failing to support the widower properly. Research shows this isn't uncommon, partners of unhealed widowers often face emotional invalidation, which can lead to self-doubt and insecurity in the relationship [20].

Finally, the tension between past and present loyalty is clear. In every story, the widower's attachment to his late wife, through rituals, memories, or emotional withdrawal, has created an ongoing imbalance. Emily and Laura's heartbreak shows the risk: even when a partner is deeply invested, supportive, and loving, unresolved grief can dominate. In Laura's case, it even ended the relationship just two weeks before Matthew's wedding anniversary to his late wife.

Wendy and James's experiences show that the imbalance can be more subtle, showing up in family expectations or ritualised loyalty, quietly eroding the partner's sense of belonging and intimacy.

Recognising these red flags isn't about blame, it's about clarity. Awareness helps partners set boundaries, seek support, and make choices that protect their emotional well-being. Unresolved grief affects more than the widower; it ripples through the relationship, shaping intimacy, emotional safety, and the partner's sense of being seen and valued. By noticing patterns like rituals, emotional withdrawal, divided loyalties, invalidation, and prioritising the past, partners can understand what's happening and take steps to safeguard themselves while navigating love and loss [4][8][20].

When a widower's late wife's memory keeps dominating family life, new partners can feel chronic emotional invalidation and experience ambiguous loss themselves by grieving a relationship that never feels complete [12][16]. Over time, this can lead to:

- Lowered self-esteem and heightened anxiety
- Resentment toward the widower or confusion

- Emotional burnout from constantly trying to prove loyalty

Grief professionals note that unresolved grief, combined with family pressures, can destabilise even long-term relationships by keeping the late spouse's presence dominant [8].

Opening the Conversation

Recognising red flags is only the first step; the next is deciding whether and how to address them. Bringing up sensitive topics with a widower requires courage, emotional intelligence, and timing. The goal is not to accuse or fix him, but to open an honest conversation about whether the relationship is truly mutual and emotionally available for growth. Grief experts remind us that avoidance often deepens disconnection, while honest communication, approached with care, can create opportunities for healing and clarity.

While these dates can evoke grief and remembrance, it's essential for new partners to be able to voice their feelings and needs without feeling guilty. Framing your thoughts with "I" statements keeps the focus on your own experience rather than assigning blame, encouraging open dialogue instead of defensiveness. Examples include:

- "I notice that around this time of year, I feel anxious and unsure of my place in your life. Can we talk about ways to navigate this week together?"
- "When we approach the anniversary of your late wife, I feel conflicted and unsure how to show my support without losing connection with you."
- "I feel sad and disconnected when your attention turns fully to your past. I want to support you, but I also need to feel included."
- "Would it help if we planned for how we'll spend time together during these dates, so I can understand your needs and limits?"
- "I want to be present and supportive, but I also need reassurance that we'll have our own space during this week. Can we plan for that?"

- "It's hard for me to hear stories about your late wife without feeling disconnected. Can we set aside some time to share memories while also focusing on our relationship?"
- "I feel overwhelmed when there's a lot of focus on the past at this time of year. Can we explore some ways to make this less stressful for both of us?"

How he responds to these statements can reveal whether the relationship has potential for mutual, emotionally present love, or whether his grief still dominates, leaving you caught between compassion and frustration. A partner who responds with openness, empathy, and willingness to discuss demonstrates that the relationship can evolve into something healthier. On the contrary, if he becomes defensive, dismisses your feelings, or insists that you "just need to be patient," it may indicate he is not yet ready to engage in a present-focused, two-way relationship fully.

Love can honour the past, but it cannot thrive when the past becomes the centre of the present. Genuine connection requires emotional availability, openness, and the willingness to build something new together. By preparing for these conversations and using the examples above, you can express your needs, set boundaries, and seek clarity, ultimately protecting your emotional well-being while supporting the relationship in a balanced, healthy way.

What to Remember

Anniversaries and memorials can trigger a widower's unresolved grief, leaving his new partner feeling invisible, sidelined, or emotionally abandoned. When the past overshadows the present, it's a red flag that he may not be fully ready for a healthy relationship. Clear boundaries, honest communication, and shared rituals are essential to protect your well-being and claim your place in the relationship.

Chapter 8 - Social Media and Memories

"I found myself wondering if posting about the past meant that he was stuck in it".

"He forgot it was his old wedding anniversary until social media reminded him".

"Seeing pictures of the love of my life in the arms of another woman multiple times a year stung".

This chapter highlights how social media can become an emotional minefield for women in a relationship with an unhealed widower. One of the common issues that turned up in discussions with others is the effects of online memorial pages, anniversary posts, and shared photos that continue to celebrate the life he shared with his late wife. These digital actions, while meaningful to the widower and his family, can trigger feelings of exclusion, insecurity, or sadness for a new partner.

The importance of open conversation about what feels respectful and what feels painful is paramount to a healthy relationship. This includes deciding whether past posts should remain visible, how to handle tagged photos, and what role memorial pages or tribute posts should play in the present relationship.

Case Study – Sarah and David

Sarah noticed that David, her widower partner, frequently posted online around special dates and anniversaries he had shared with his late wife, sharing messages such as "Missing the love of my life," "Soulmates forever," and "Until we meet again." While heartfelt, these posts highlighted his past, leaving Sarah feeling awkward and uneasy.

His constant public displays of affection for his late wife made Sarah feel invisible, as if she were living in the shadows or occupying a third-place role in the relationship. The lack of acknowledgment or validation of their connection and relationship online caused her to question her importance in his life. When Sarah spoke to David about her concerns, he defended his right to post what he wants online and accused her of being insensitive and disrespectful.

Witnessing ongoing declarations of love for someone who had passed, while trying to build a new relationship, created tension, self-doubt, and isolation for Sarah. Ultimately, she noticed other red flags and made the difficult decision to end the relationship, recognising that David was still actively grieving his late wife.

Case Study - Emily's Story

Emily's partner frequently shared throwback photos and videos of holidays he'd taken with his late wife. While Emily understood these were cherished memories, she admitted that each new post stirred feelings of inadequacy, isolation and embarrassment. His friends and family would comment on how perfect the late couple had been together and how hard it was to bear her passing, without acknowledging that he had found love again.

Over time, Emily found it increasingly difficult to voice her discomfort, worried that speaking up might seem selfish or unsympathetic. She had found ways to cope with the shrine, the photos, and the difficulties around his old anniversary dates, but his social media posts, public displays of love for another woman, felt impossible to reconcile. Feeling secondary to his past life and hurt that her needs were neither acknowledged nor understood, Emily ultimately recognised that the weight of his ongoing grief was too heavy for her to carry. Despite her love for him, she made the painful decision to end the relationship, realising she could not maintain her own emotional well-being while remaining in a partnership where she felt invisible and overshadowed by his past life.

Case Study - Shelby's Story

Shelby noticed that her partner's friends and family would frequently comment on and share memories of special occasions he had celebrated with his late wife, such as anniversaries, birthdays, and holidays. They posted heartfelt messages and reminisced openly, but when it came to milestones in Shelby and her partner's current relationship, there was silence. Their new anniversaries and shared memories were never acknowledged online. Shelby felt hurt and invisible, as if her relationship was less valid or meaningful.

This unequal recognition amplified her sense of isolation and made her question whether she truly belonged in the widower's life. It also highlighted to Shelby how social media can unintentionally reinforce the emotional distance between a widower's past and present relationships.

Case Study - Lyn and Warren

After remarrying, Warren posted photos from his wedding day on social media, excited to share this new chapter of his life. While a few acquaintances offered polite congratulations, most family members and longtime friends either ignored the post or shared old memories of his late wife instead. The lack of support and acknowledgment left Lyn feeling deeply hurt and isolated. She felt as though the new marriage was overshadowed by the continued public devotion to Warren's late wife.

Warren could not see what the problem was, as he thought that the social media posts related to his late wife were respectful to his past life and not disrespectful to his current one. Lyn decided to mute her new husband's social media account around these dates to avoid further uncomfortable moments as she struggled to understand public emotional divides between past and present relationships.

Recognising the Red Flags

Across multiple case studies, a clear pattern emerges when a widower maintains frequent digital or social connections to his late wife, the emotional impact on the new partner can be profound. In Sarah and David's story, public love for the deceased, combined with defensiveness when concerns were raised, left Sarah feeling invisible and caught in a three-way dynamic. Similarly, Emily's partner frequently shared memories of past holidays with his late wife, and praise from friends and family reinforced her sense of inadequacy and disconnection. Both women ultimately ended their relationships, recognising that unresolved grief had taken precedence over their emotional needs.

Shelby's experience highlights another subtle but damaging dynamic: milestones of the widower's past were celebrated while the new relationship's achievements went unacknowledged. This imbalance left her questioning her place in his life and reinforced feelings of isolation. Even well-intentioned actions, such as Warren posting about a new marriage while still honouring his late wife, can leave a new partner feeling overshadowed, hurt, or excluded, particularly when family and friends continue to prioritise the deceased.

The common thread across these cases is consistent:

- Frequent online memorialisation or sharing of past memories.
- Lack of acknowledgment of the current relationship.
- Dismissal of the new partner's feelings.
- Reinforcement of the deceased's memory by social circles.

These dynamics can foster confusion, self-doubt, and emotional isolation, sometimes contributing to relationship breakdown. When grief remains unresolved, digitally or socially, the new partner's emotional needs are often sidelined, which can leave her feeling unseen, undervalued, and insecure.

Professional insight reinforces these observations. Psychologists and grief experts note that digital memorials, tribute posts, and frequent sharing of photos of a late spouse can complicate grief and create tension in new relationships [7][9][17]. Dr Pauline Boss explains that a deceased partner's ongoing digital presence can keep grief unresolved for the widower while intensifying exclusion for the new partner [9]. Therapist Megan Devine highlights that while grief requires space, couples must establish boundaries so new love can grow without feeling overshadowed [7].

Research on continuing bonds shows that frequent posts about a late spouse can unintentionally signal that the deceased remains the central emotional focus, potentially eroding trust and belonging for a new partner [4][17]. Open discussions about what types of posts feel supportive versus painful, how frequently to share, and whether to archive older content can create space for the present relationship while still honouring the past.

Friends and family may be reluctant to openly recognise a widower's new partner, worried it could feel disrespectful to the deceased. When the widower does not validate his partner's feelings, address her emotional needs, or set digital and social boundaries with himself, his friends, family, and even former in-laws, he is neglecting the needs of the relationship. This can amplify her sense of invisibility, create ongoing tension, and place additional strain on trust, intimacy, and the couple's shared sense of identity.

Opening the Conversation

Navigating a widower's digital presence can be challenging for a new partner. Photos, throwbacks, tagged posts, and public declarations of love for a late spouse can stir feelings of inadequacy, invisibility, or emotional displacement. These experiences are valid, and addressing them openly can help protect your emotional well-being while clarifying the boundaries of your relationship.

If you notice digital patterns that make you feel sidelined or uncomfortable, consider beginning the conversation, and keep the focus on your experience rather than on blame. For example:

- "Seeing posts where you publicly express love for another woman leaves me feeling secondary. Can we discuss how your social media can reflect our relationship, too?"

- "I understand anniversaries and special dates are meaningful for you. I want to be supportive, but I also need to express that seeing these dates highlighted online can be difficult for me. How can we navigate this together?"

- "I notice that some of your posts about your late wife leave me feeling disconnected from you. Can we talk about ways to share memories without me feeling invisible?"

- "When I see photos or posts celebrating your late wife online, I feel sad and unsure how to engage. Could we agree on boundaries for social media?"

- "Seeing public messages or tagged posts about your late wife sometimes makes me feel secondary. I want to discuss ways for our relationship also to be recognised."

- "I feel anxious when your late wife's memory is shared publicly without considering my feelings.

Can we talk about what's important for both of us?"

- "I want to support you and honour the past, but I also need my emotional needs acknowledged. Can we discuss guidelines for social media around your past relationship?"

- "When posts about your late wife appear, I feel a mix of sadness and insecurity. Could we explore ways to balance remembering her while nurturing our relationship?"

Friends and family may be reluctant to openly recognise a widower's new partner, worried it could feel disrespectful to the deceased. When the widower does not validate his partner's feelings or address her emotional needs, this can amplify her sense of invisibility and place additional strain on trust, intimacy, and the couple's shared sense of identity.

How he responds in these moments tells you everything. If he can listen openly, show empathy, and discuss boundaries without shutting down, there is room for a mutually emotionally present relationship.

If he becomes defensive, dismissive, or minimises your feelings, it's often a sign that grief is still running the relationship, leaving you stuck between compassion for his loss and frustration for yourself. At that point, it's not just about patience or understanding, but about protecting your own emotional safety.

What to Remember

Social media posts and digital memorials can unintentionally keep a widower's grief at the forefront, potentially leaving the new partner feeling invisible or sidelined. Open communication, clear boundaries, and shared understanding help honour the past without overshadowing the present. When managed thoughtfully, these strategies turn potential conflict into trust, respect, and emotional connection.

Chapter 9 – That's Not My Name

"We were being intimate, and he called me by her name".

"My kids were not happy when he said "we" or "us" in some of the stories that he told, as it gave them the impression that our relationship started before it did, meaning that I cheated on their dad when clearly, I didn't".

"It hurt when he called me her name; he always apologised, but I still wondered what he was thinking about".

In this chapter, we explore why some widowers accidentally call their new partners by their late wife's name, and why they use words like "we," "us," and "our" when speaking about shared experiences from their past marriage. This language can be confusing and painful for the new partner, reinforcing a sense of being an outsider in the relationship. Drawing on professional insights and real-life stories, this chapter shows that while the use of past-focused language helps the widower keep the memory of his late wife alive, it can unintentionally distance and unsettle the partner who is meant to be part of the present.

Widowers may unconsciously hold onto couple-based language because their identity was built over years of shared experiences. According to grief expert Dr Susan J. Elliott [8], these habits come from a place of attachment and memory, rather than an intention to hurt the new partner.

Personally, I would have been more comfortable if Bill had used his late wife's name rather than "we" and "our" or "my wife" when he wasn't referring to us, as he unintentionally reinforced a painful sense of being an outsider in my own relationship.

There was one moment that stands out clearly. Two members of the fire brigade visited our property to discuss a controlled burn and possible access through the neighbour's driveway. While answering their questions, Bill casually mentioned that the neighbours had once given his wife a hard time. Both firefighters turned to me immediately, assuming he meant *me*, and one of them began directing sympathetic questions in my direction.

Caught off guard, I had to clarify that I wasn't Bill's wife. One firefighter glanced at my bare ring finger, then back at me with a quietly disapproving look. Suddenly, I was aware of how easily outsiders could misunderstand our situation, and how quickly I could be judged as "the other woman."

Flustered and embarrassed, I blurted out that Bill's wife had passed away. The firefighters offered their condolences to Bill, but the damage had already been done. Long after they left, the feeling of humiliation lingered, another reminder that even in my own relationship, I felt like I was competing with someone who was no longer here.

Many women share that certain words can signal a widower's ongoing attachment to his late wife, affecting the new partner's emotional footing. Finding compassionate language helps honour the past while creating space for a new "us" to grow.

Case Study: Donna and Joel

Donna and her partner, Joel, a widower, were a social couple and often visited new places to meet new people. When spending time with new acquaintances, Joel would often say things that reflected his past life, such as "We loved that restaurant" or "It's our favourite place." Donna would pause, trying to recall whether they had visited those places together, only to realise that Joel was referring to memories with his late wife. These moments created awkwardness, leaving Donna feeling invisible and excluded from the shared narrative.

Even more challenging, new acquaintances sometimes misunderstood, assuming Joel's wife was still alive and that Donna was involved with a married man. She often felt humiliated, needing to explain that Joel's wife had passed away and that she wasn't the "other woman." The confusion deepened when Joel continued to refer to his late wife simply as "my wife," rather than "my late wife," reinforcing assumptions that caused discomfort for them both.

Case Study: Melanie and Max

Melanie had been dating Max, a widower, for over a year. Max had shared a long marriage with his late wife, and sometimes this would come through in subtle but painful ways for Melanie. When they were out with Max's friends or family, Max would occasionally use phrases like "we loved this spot" or "we love our favourite holiday place," referring to experiences he had with his late wife.

Melanie found these moments confusing and hurtful. She would sometimes freeze, unsure whether Max was talking about a memory with her or with his late wife. The discomfort grew when she noticed others glance awkwardly at her, realising Max was reminiscing about someone else. Melanie began to feel like an outsider in her own relationship, overshadowed by the memory of a woman she had never met.

In private, Melanie tried to explain to Max how the language affected her. Max felt defensive at first, explaining that these habits were deeply ingrained from years of marriage. Over time, they worked together to find new ways of speaking, using "I" instead of "we" or clarifying when he was sharing a memory from the past, to help Melanie feel more secure and included in their life together.

Case Study – Sally and Simon

Sally had been seeing Simon for over a year. His late wife, Mandy, had passed away three years earlier. At first, Sally excused Simon's repeated slips of calling her "Mandy" as muscle memory, but over time, it became increasingly hurtful, especially when he accidentally called her Mandy during intimate moments.

The situation reached a breaking point at a public function when Simon referred to Sally as "Mandy" in front of several people and made no attempt to correct himself. Many guests assumed Sally was Mandy, forcing her to repeatedly clarify that she was not Mandy and to explain who Mandy actually was. The experience left her feeling humiliated, invisible, and deeply unsettled.

Sally boldly asked Simon if he was still grieving. He told her that he would always grieve his late wife and think about her, a statement that left Sally feeling simultaneously understanding and yet profoundly aware of the emotional barrier it created between them. Sally tried to explain to Simon how confusing and painful this behaviour was, but he brushed it off, insisting it was "just a slip of the tongue." Seeking perspective, she spoke to a friend, who suggested that Simon might have stored her name alongside Mandy's in his mind, a possible reflection of the depth of his love for his late wife and Sally.

Rather than feeling honoured or included, Sally felt embarrassed, hurt, and bewildered. Being called Mandy, particularly in front of others, made her feel sidelined and invisible, and was a stark reminder of how a widower's unresolved grief can seep into a new relationship. When Sally shared how confusing and painful it was that Simon used "we" and "us" to mean himself and his late wife, Simon apologised but added that he couldn't change who he was or how he spoke about "the love of his life." This left Sally feeling even more hurt, unseen, and uncertain about her place in Simon's heart.

Recognising the Red Flags

Being in a relationship with an unhealed widower can feel confusing, emotionally taxing, and at times disorienting, particularly when grief from the past subtly, or overtly, intrudes into the present. Across multiple stories, clear patterns emerge, certain behaviours, language choices, and interaction habits signal that unresolved grief may be shaping the widower's emotional availability and affecting the relationship's dynamics.

In Donna and Joel's case, Joel frequently used "we" and "our" when recalling experiences with his late wife. Donna often felt invisible, awkward, and forced to clarify that she wasn't "the other woman." Similarly, Melanie felt a persistent ache when Max referred to past experiences with his late wife using "we" and "us." By discussing her feelings, Melanie and Max found ways to adjust his language, using "I" when speaking about the past, which helped her feel acknowledged and included.

Sally's experience highlights a more overt red flag: being called her partner's late wife's name, sometimes even in public, without apologies or correction. Despite expressing her discomfort, Simon dismissed her concerns, insisting he couldn't change the way he spoke about "the love of his life." This revealed his ongoing emotional attachment and left Sally feeling unseen, marginalised, and unsure of her place in the relationship.

It's important to recognise that many of these behaviours are often unintentional. Cognitive psychologists describe this as a form of muscle memory: over time, the brain encodes repeated habits, routines, and patterns of speech into neural pathways, making them almost automatic [45]. For a widower, calling a new partner by the late wife's name or using "we" when referring to shared experiences with the deceased is usually reflex, not deliberate. While anyone might slip up occasionally, like calling a child by the wrong name, when these patterns repeat without being acknowledged, they can leave the new partner feeling sidelined, invisible, or forced to compete against a memory.

For the widower, understanding how grief and muscle memory shape these habits opens doors to change. For the new partner, recognising these patterns brings clarity, confidence, and the ability to assert her place in the relationship without guilt.

Ultimately, recognising red flags isn't about blame. It's about understanding how grief quietly shapes the emotional landscape and learning to navigate the tension between past and present. By paying attention to these signals, both partners can honour memory while ensuring that unresolved grief does not overshadow, dominate, or marginalise their new relationship.

Opening the Conversation

When a widower uses "we" or "us" to refer to experiences with his late wife or calls the new partner by his late wife's name, it can feel painfully uncomfortable and disorienting. While these habits are often unintentional, they can leave the new partner feeling sidelined, invisible, or as if they are competing with a memory. Approaching the conversation thoughtfully can help both partners gain understanding and ease the emotional strain.

- "I feel confused and invisible when I hear 'we' or 'our' used for experiences that don't include me."

- "I feel hurt and overlooked when I'm called your late wife's name. It makes me question my place in your life."

- "When you say 'we' or 'our,' who are you thinking of?"

- "Can you help me understand what it feels like for you when these names or phrases come out?"

- "I understand these slips are likely unintentional, but it would mean a lot if you could pause and correct yourself when it happens."
- "Can we agree on a way to talk about your memories that keeps me feeling included?"

If these patterns continue and cause ongoing tension, it may signal red flags or indicate unresolved grief is affecting the relationship. Ultimately, the goal is to foster emotional clarity, respect, and inclusion. By addressing these subtle but impactful habits, partners can build a stronger, more secure relationship where memories of the past are honoured without overshadowing the present connection.

What to Remember

Hearing "we", "us" or "our" for past experiences, or being called by his late wife's name, can feel confusing and hurtful. Occasional slips may be harmless, but repeated patterns that leave you feeling invisible or sidelined signal that his grief may still be active and he may not yet be fully present in the relationship.

Chapter 10 – Reaching out to the Other Side

"He wanted to stay connected to her at all costs."

"I felt creeped out when I found that he visited a medium"

"I felt that his need to seek guidance from his late wife was weird. I never knew what to say"

In this chapter, we will explore why some widowers turn to spiritual practices such as tarot readings and visits to mediums as a way of coping with their grief. For some widowers, these practices can initially seem comforting, offering a sense of continued connection with a past life. However, for an unhealed widower, these practices can keep them emotionally anchored in the past, making it harder to invest fully in a new relationship.

Psychologically, this fixation often stems from unresolved grief, feelings of guilt, and a desperate need for reassurance that the late wife approves of the new life he is building. According to Neimeyer [16], such behaviours can also be attempts to manage anxiety about loss and mortality.

When a widower frequently seeks contact with their late spouse through mediums or tarot card readers, it can leave their new partner feeling confused, excluded and emotionally displaced. The thought of maintaining a spiritual bond with a deceased partner is a deeply personal one, and for some, it can provide a sense of peace. However, when that focus becomes central, it risks eroding intimacy, trust, and emotional safety in the new relationship.

Couples facing this situation must talk openly about their feelings, establish boundaries that respect both partners' needs. Healing after loss involves integrating the past, not living in it, and without that balance, the living partner can begin to feel invisible in their own relationship.

Case Study – Mark and Olivia

Mark, a widower in his late fifties, had been with Olivia for almost a year when she learned he regularly visited a medium who claimed to channel messages from his late wife. At first, Olivia respected these sessions as part of his healing, believing that everyone grieves differently. But over time, the sessions began to cast a shadow over their relationship.

Mark often invited Olivia to listen to the recordings. The medium would refer to his late wife as *his wife* and *the love of his life*, never acknowledging Olivia or their relationship. Each session left Olivia feeling like an outsider, reminded that she could never truly step into his heart.

Instead of bringing comfort, the visits deepened Mark's sadness and emotional withdrawal. When Olivia expressed her unease, Mark insisted the sessions helped him, though he couldn't explain why he needed them so often. His silence left her feeling increasingly excluded and uncertain about their future.

As time passed, Olivia realised that while Mark's body was in the present, his spirit remained tethered to the past. No matter how much she loved him, she could not compete with the memory of a woman he still considered his true soulmate. Eventually, Olivia accepted that she was living in the shadow of a love that death had not ended, and she quietly walked away.

Case Study – Gordon and Stacy

Gordon and Stacy had been together for three years, living under the same roof for twelve months, and married for just six. From the outside, theirs appeared to be a settled, loving partnership built on shared history and the excitement of building a future together. But an unexpected discovery shattered Stacy's sense of security.

While reviewing their shared bank account statements, Stacy noticed recurring payments to several online tarot card readers. At first, she felt confused, even slightly guilty for snooping, but her confusion soon turned to hurt as she pieced together that these sessions always took place near significant dates tied to Gordon's late wife: her birthday, the anniversary of her passing, and even his old wedding anniversary.

Unable to ignore what she'd found, Stacy confronted Gordon gently but directly. She asked why he felt the need to contact tarot readers and what exactly he was searching for. After some hesitation, Gordon admitted that he wanted reassurance that his late wife was "still around," and more painfully, that she approved of the choices he was making in his new life, including his relationship with Stacy.

What shocked Stacy most was Gordon's next admission: before proposing to her, he had consulted his favourite tarot reader to see if his late wife "approved" of him remarrying. Stacy, stunned, asked him what he would have done if the tarot card reader had said no. Gordon, after a pause, answered honestly: "Probably wouldn't have asked you to marry me."

That single statement landed heavily on Stacy's heart. Suddenly, the story of their engagement, a moment she'd cherished as a symbol of his love and commitment, felt reframed. Instead of an act of love freely chosen, it now felt conditional, as if filtered through a conversation Gordon was still having with his late wife.

Though Gordon assured Stacy that the tarot reader had confirmed his late wife's blessing, this explanation offered little comfort. Instead, it left Stacy with even more questions.

In the days that followed, Stacy wrestled with painful realisations. Their marriage, which she had believed to be a promise between two people in the present, now felt intertwined with someone who belonged to Gordon's past but still influenced his most intimate decisions. The tarot readings were not merely harmless rituals; they had been shaping major moments in their life together, without her knowledge or participation.

For Stacy, this discovery was more than unsettling; it was deeply destabilising. It made her question not just Gordon's commitment, but also whether he was truly emotionally present in their marriage, or still living, in part, under the guidance and shadow of the woman he had loved and lost.

Recognising the Red Flags

These stories reveal how unresolved grief can quietly shape, and ultimately strain, a new relationship. Although each widower expressed his grief differently, the emotional outcome for their partners was strikingly similar: both women felt excluded, uncertain, and haunted by the invisible presence of another woman who continued to influence their partner's heart and choices.

Mark regularly visited a medium who channelled messages from his late wife, while Gordon turned to tarot readers seeking her "approval", even before proposing to Stacy. Both men, in different ways, remained emotionally tethered to their past marriages, allowing a projection to hold power over decisions in their current relationships.

For Olivia, Mark's medium sessions deepened his sadness and emotional withdrawal, leaving her feeling isolated and unseen. For Stacy, learning that Gordon's proposal was influenced by a tarot reader's "message" from his late wife shattered her sense of security. In both cases, love in the present became overshadowed by loyalty to the past.

Professionals in grief and bereavement psychology, such as Neimeyer [16] and Worden [4], note that when widowers continue seeking contact or approval from their late wife through mediums, tarot, or rituals, it may indicate unresolved grief or guilt. These behaviours often serve as a way to gain reassurance or permission to move forward. While such practices might momentarily comfort the widower, they can leave the living partner feeling secondary, spiritually and emotionally displaced.

As grief expert David Kessler reminds us: *"Healing doesn't mean forgetting the person who died; it means finding a place for them where they don't stop you from loving the living."* [2]. When a widower's continued spiritual contact with his late wife takes precedence over his current partner's comfort or beliefs, it becomes a significant red flag. What may begin as an innocent or private act of remembrance can quietly erode trust and intimacy. The living partner may begin to feel excluded, competing not with another woman, but with the memory of one.

Opening the Conversation

Recognising the red flags is the first step; the next is deciding whether and how to address them. Bringing up sensitive topics with a widower requires courage, empathy, and timing. The goal is not to accuse or fix him, but to open an honest conversation about how his actions, whether spiritual contact, rituals, or other expressions of loyalty to his late wife, affect your sense of security, belonging, and emotional well-being. Here are some conversation starter examples...

- "I feel excluded and anxious when you consult a medium or tarot reader about your late wife. I want to support you, but I also need to feel included and safe in our relationship."

- "When you perform rituals or speak of messages from your late wife, I feel unsure of my place. Can we talk about how to balance remembering her with being present together?"

- "I feel hurt when decisions in our relationship seem influenced by messages or signs from the past. Can we discuss how to honour your late wife without overshadowing us?"

- "It's difficult for me when I feel like I'm competing with the memory of your late wife. Can you help me understand how you experience this, and how we can navigate it together?"

- "I want to support your grieving process, but I also need to know that our relationship is valued in the present. Can we explore ways to do both?"

- "I notice that some of your spiritual practices leave me feeling unseen. Can we find a way for you to honour her that doesn't make me feel secondary?"

The aim is to foster understanding, emotional clarity, and mutual respect. Opening the conversation in a calm, thoughtful way allows both partners to communicate their feelings, set boundaries, and work toward a balance in which past memories are honoured while the present relationship can grow and flourish.

Recognising this pattern is essential. These moments often signal that grief has not yet been integrated and that emotional energy remains invested in the past. Relationships grounded in the present require both partners to be emotionally available. When one partner's heart remains anchored to someone who has died, the new relationship cannot grow, no matter how much love or patience the other brings.

What to Remember

Physical presence without emotional presence is still a form of absence. True intimacy cannot grow when a relationship is guided by voices from the past rather than shared choices in the present.

Chapter 11 – The Shadows of a Bad Marriage

"I kept asking myself what I did wrong, why he didn't trust me — until I realised the betrayal he was really fighting happened long before I ever met him."

"It's like living with someone whose heart is still arguing with a ghost, and I'm just caught in the crossfire."

"At first, he made me feel chosen and special, like I was finally part of his new beginning. But over time, it felt like every argument was really about her, not me."

In this chapter, we examine a challenging dynamic: relationships in which the widower experienced conflict or unhappiness in his previous marriage. Unresolved emotions from that past relationship, such as anger, guilt, or regret, may resurface, either subtly or overtly, shaping his behaviour and the emotional landscape of his new partnership.

Women I've spoken with often describe how these unresolved feelings can manifest as criticism or comparisons to the late wife, mood swings, emotional withdrawal, sarcasm, or even self-sabotaging behaviours. The new partner may feel punished for mistakes that aren't hers or become an unintended outlet for the widower's unresolved pain. These patterns can leave her feeling confused, hurt, and unsure of her place in the relationship.

Professional insight reinforces these observations. Dr Susan J. Elliott notes that when unresolved anger or regret from a previous marriage goes unprocessed, it can create tension, miscommunication, and emotional invalidation in new partnerships [8]. Such behaviours often stem from a psychological struggle between the widower's desire for connection and his fear of repeating past pain.

Case studies and conversations with women bring these patterns out of theory and into real life. A widower may replay unresolved dynamics from his previous marriage, meet conflict with coldness or sarcasm, or withdraw emotionally, and sometimes physically, when things become uncomfortable. At times, guilt or regret is quietly projected onto the new relationship, slowly eroding its stability.

Recognising these signs early is crucial. Setting healthy boundaries, fostering open and honest communication, and acknowledging when a widower may need time to process past hurts are essential steps toward building a safe and mutually fulfilling relationship. Awareness, rather than blame, empowers the new partner to protect her emotional well-being while supporting the widower's journey toward healing.

Case Study: Emma and Richard

Emma began dating Richard, a widower who was initially affectionate, kind, and seemed eager to build a future together. Over time, Richard shared that his late wife had been emotionally abusive and had cheated on him multiple times. Emma felt sympathy and wanted to support him through his pain.

However, after the first few months, Richard's behaviour began to change. He became increasingly critical, questioning Emma's choices and accusing her of having hidden motives. Small disagreements would escalate into heated arguments where Richard blamed Emma for things she didn't do, echoing patterns from his past marriage. Emma found herself constantly confused and questioning her own behaviour, wondering if she was somehow at fault.

Despite Emma's efforts to reassure him and communicate openly, Richard's unresolved anger and hurt from his late wife's betrayal seemed to spill over into their relationship. His mood swings left Emma feeling as if she were walking on eggshells, and she struggled with guilt and anxiety, wondering why she couldn't make him feel secure.

Case Study: Claire and Jonathan

Claire had been in a relationship with Jonathan, a widower, for two years before she began noticing troubling changes. At first, Jonathan had been warm, affectionate, and deeply appreciative of Claire's kindness. But slowly, a darker pattern emerged: Jonathan would sometimes shut down completely, giving Claire the silent treatment for days at a time. At other times, seemingly out of nowhere, he would lash out verbally, criticising her appearance or opinions, or accusing her of insensitivity to his loss.

Claire was left in shock and disbelief, as these episodes were unpredictable and out of character compared to the early days of their relationship. Despite her attempts to discuss how the behaviour made her feel, Jonathan often flipped the conversation, suggesting

Claire was too demanding or not understanding enough.

Over time, Claire felt as though she was being punished for mistakes she hadn't made, carrying the emotional burden of conflicts grounded in Jonathan's unresolved anger and guilt from his past marriage. Claire decided to tell Johnathan how she felt, and he responded by ending the relationship.

Recognising the Red Flags

Relationships with unhealed widowers can be confusing and emotionally challenging, particularly when unresolved grief, guilt, or trauma from a past marriage seeps into the present. Both case studies of Richard and Jonathan illustrate this: initially appearing caring and ready to rebuild their lives, each widower's unresolved pain eventually surfaced in destructive behaviours. Richard expressed his grief through accusations and escalating criticism, while Jonathan used silent treatment and unpredictable verbal attacks. Their partners, Emma and Claire, were left questioning their own actions and worth, despite not being the source of the pain. In these cases, the new partner can unintentionally carry the emotional consequences of a widower's unprocessed grief and hurt.

These dynamics show how a widower's unresolved grief or past marital conflict can unintentionally seep into a new relationship, colouring interactions in ways he may not fully recognise. As outlined by the American Psychiatric Association, ongoing exposure to destabilising behaviours, such as criticism, blame-shifting, or emotional inconsistency, can lead to increased anxiety, depressive symptoms, diminished confidence, and a constant sense of needing to be on guard [20].

According to grief and relationship experts, unhealed widowers may unintentionally project anger, regret, or frustration onto a new partner, creating cycles of self-doubt, guilt, and confusion, while eroding emotional safety, trust, and stability [8]. Repeated negative patterns, if left unaddressed, cannot be healed by love alone. Professional guidance, open communication, and the establishment of clear boundaries are essential to protect one's mental and emotional well-being.

It is also important to recognise that some widowers may present narratives about their past marriage that are inaccurate or skewed. Stories of difficult or unhappy relationships may be used, consciously or unconsciously, to elicit sympathy, deflect accountability, or maintain control. While these behaviours do not automatically indicate narcissism, patterns of distortion, self-victimisation, or emotional manipulation, they can overlap with narcissistic traits [20]. Dr Craig Malkin, author of *Rethinking Narcissism*, notes that encountering these patterns can provoke confusion, guilt, and emotional strain, particularly for partners who have experienced prior emotionally challenging relationships [21].

Remember, recognising red flags is not about blaming the widower, it's about helping you understand what is happening in the relationship and protecting your own emotional well-being. Being aware of patterns that may signal unresolved grief or unhealthy behaviours allows you to set boundaries, seek support when needed, and make informed choices. This perspective empowers you to care for yourself while navigating the balance between compassion for your partner's loss and ensuring that your own needs are seen, valued, and respected.

Opening the Conversation

When a widower describes having had a difficult or unhappy marriage with his late wife, it can be especially confusing if his behaviour in the new relationship begins to mirror the very patterns he claimed caused him distress in the past. Raised voices, criticism, blame-shifting, emotional withdrawal, or volatility may leave you questioning why those behaviours recur or why they are now directed at you. These moments can be confronting, and they can signal unresolved conflict, trauma, or unprocessed grief from the widower's previous relationship.

Opening a conversation about these concerns requires clarity, calm, and emotional self-respect. The aim is not to accuse, but to express how the behaviour impacts you and to understand whether he is willing to take responsibility for how past wounds are affecting the present. Here are some examples:

- "I feel unsettled when you speak about how unhappy your past marriage was, but some of those same behaviours are happening between us. I'd like to understand what's going on."
- "When I'm blamed or criticised in ways that sound similar to stories you've shared about your past relationship, I feel confused and emotionally unsafe. Can we talk about this pattern?"
- "I feel anxious when past conflicts seem to spill into our relationship. I want us to discuss how we can separate old pain from what we're building together."
- "When the way you speak to me echoes the frustrations you described with your late wife, it leaves me feeling responsible for things that

aren't mine to carry. Can we explore why this is happening?"

- "I want to support your healing, but I also need to feel respected and emotionally secure. Can we talk about how your past relationship may still be influencing your reactions?"

- "I hear that your previous marriage was difficult. When similar behaviours surface now, I feel worried about the direction we're heading. How can we address this together?"

When conversations are repeatedly met with denial, dismissal, or defensiveness, it's often less about the topic at hand and more about what hasn't yet been faced. Unprocessed grief, unresolved trauma, or long-standing relationship patterns tend to surface this way, not loudly, but persistently. These patterns are not yours to absorb or repair. Simply recognising them matters.

A healthy relationship requires emotional presence, accountability, and respect in the here and now. Anything less risks allowing the past to quietly steer the present, asking you to accommodate wounds that were never yours to carry.

What to Remember

When widowers carry unresolved anger and guilt into a new relationship, love alone often isn't enough to heal the past. Recognising these patterns and seeking help protects both partners from repeating old wounds. It is not the responsibility of the new partner to identify and/ or assist a widower to come to terms with his past relationship.

Chapter 12 - The Shadow of Her Belongings

"He didn't want to change anything."

"Her clothes were still hanging behind the door".

"He gave me her clothes and would often ask me why I didn't wear them."

In this chapter, we explore how a widower's attachment to his late wife's belongings and favourite things can unintentionally create emotional distance in his new relationship. These lingering connections often appear in everyday life, a jacket still hanging in the wardrobe, familiar ornaments in shared spaces, or gentle suggestions that his new partner use items that once belonged to his late wife.

We'll examine why widowers may struggle to release these tangible reminders of the past and how this can leave a new partner feeling overshadowed or secondary. Experts emphasise the importance of balancing respect for the past with the creation of new, shared memories.

From my own experience, I noticed that Bill found it difficult to part with his late wife's belongings. Though he no longer needed them and no one in his or his late wife's family wanted them, he kept them out of a mix of respect and guilt; he couldn't bear the thought of giving them away. Grief expert James Worden notes that objects, routines, and familiar places often serve as "continuing bonds," helping widowers maintain a sense of connection to the deceased [4]. For Bill, these items soothed his guilt and fear of letting go, yet they also tethered him to the past. The idea of minimising them felt like an act of betrayal.

Psychologists explain that this kind of behaviour is often linked to attachment. As John Bowlby describes, the bond formed with a spouse is a deep emotional anchor, and when that bond is broken, the surviving partner often looks for ways to stay connected, even if only symbolically [29]. Physical items like clothing, photos, or favourite pieces of furniture can become emotional bridges, offering comfort in the absence of the person who once gave their world meaning.

For many widowers, these belongings act as transitional objects, something familiar that helps them feel close to their late wife. It's rarely intentional, more an instinctive attempt to preserve a sense of security and continuity when everything else has been disrupted. Research by Stroebe and Schut helps shed light on why this happens. Their *Dual Process Model of Grief* explains that people naturally move between two states: one in which they face their loss head-on (loss-oriented coping), and another in which they focus on everyday life to avoid the pain (restoration-oriented coping) [5]. Keeping belongings visible can be a quiet way of avoiding the full pain of loss, a kind of emotional buffer that helps them function day to day. But when this pattern continues over time, it can unintentionally create emotional distance, making it harder for a widower to truly invest in a new relationship.

Dr Robert Neimeyer also notes that personal items play a role in meaning reconstruction after loss: they help widowers sustain continuity and identity, especially when life feels fragmented. Letting go of these items can feel like letting go of a part of themselves or their history [16]. This explains why even years later, some widowers feel paralysed by guilt, fear, or the belief that discarding belongings equates to erasing the person they loved.

Widowers who hold tightly to these reminders, keeping clothing and personal items visible or revisiting sentimental places, can inadvertently make their new partner feel like a visitor in someone else's life. The constant presence of Bill's late wife's belongings made it difficult for me to create a home that felt like ours. At times, I felt more like a caretaker of his memories than a cherished partner. It took nearly two years for Bill to be ready to move most of her belongings into storage. Although he had no children, I often thought about how, if he passed away first, I would be left to manage another woman's memories, a responsibility I did not want.

At the heart of it, these behaviours usually come from unresolved attachment and fear of loss, not from a desire to hurt. Physical reminders, photos, keepsakes, and routines can be comforting, but leaning on them too heavily can quietly hold back a new relationship. In my own experience, I spent a lot of time walking that tightrope: trying to honour his past while carving out a present that genuinely felt like ours.

Case Study- Brian and Ruby

Brian and Ruby were together for two years when they decided to move in together. Ruby sold her home and contributed some of the proceeds to renovate Brian's house to create space for all their children.

Ruby naively believed that, over time, Brian would make space in the master bedroom for her belongings and personal items. Instead, he kept his late wife's belongings untouched and visible, citing the children's comfort as the reason. Ruby found herself with only a hallway storage cupboard for her clothes, making her feel excluded and overshadowed within the shared home they were supposed to build together.

This imbalance of emotional and physical space led to feelings of sadness, frustration, and questioning her place in the relationship. Ruby tried to communicate her feelings of discomfort with Brian, but he always responded with reasons such as "I'm doing this for my children" and "It's not that important". Eventually, the dismissal of Ruby's needs and concerns caused severe damage to their relationship, and Ruby and her children moved out into a rental. Ruby regretted selling her home and moving in with Brian. Ruby went to counselling, and Brian joined an online dating site.

Case Study – Adrian and Mandy

Adrian sold the home he had shared with his late wife and moved into his new partner Mandy's brand-new house. With him came a desire to bring many of his late wife's cherished possessions. Mandy, wanting their home to feel balanced and shared, gently suggested he keep a small keepsake box and pass the rest on to his adult children. Adrian resisted, feeling that giving away those items would dishonour his late wife's memory. He explained that his children didn't want more of their mother's belongings; he had already passed on many things before.

This disagreement created an undercurrent of tension that ran through much of their five-year relationship. Mandy became increasingly overwhelmed by the sheer number of reminders of Adrian's late wife throughout the house. Instead of feeling like an equal partner, she often felt like a guest in a space that was supposed to be her own.

The turning point came when Adrian unpacked his late wife's wedding dress and hung it in the walk-in wardrobe, telling Mandy he was "used to seeing it every day." To Mandy, it felt like walking into a moment frozen in time, a reminder that she was sharing her home and her relationship with a ghost she could never compete with. Adrian's grief was real, but so was its impact. His inability to let go, while understandable, slowly consumed the emotional room needed for them to build a future together.

It didn't end there. Adrian insisted on decorating the shared living spaces with his late wife's favourite décor, despite Mandy's gentle efforts to introduce pieces that reflected the life *they* were trying to create. The final fracture came when he set up a new shrine, complete with photos and her ashes, while Mandy was out visiting friends. She returned to find a memorial taking pride of place in her lounge room, a quiet but powerful message that the past still held priority over the present.

Their relationship ultimately didn't survive. Mandy wasn't competing with another woman; she was competing with grief, nostalgia, and a version of Adrian that still belonged to someone else.

Recognising the Red Flags

The stories of Brian and Ruby, and Adrian and Mandy, reveal how a widower's attachment to his late wife's belongings can quietly, and sometimes painfully, shape the emotional landscape of a new relationship. What begins as an act of respect or sentiment can evolve into a barrier, leaving the new partner feeling excluded, overshadowed, and emotionally displaced.

In Brian and Ruby's case, the imbalance was both emotional and physical. Ruby moved into Brian's home, believing they would create a shared space; yet his late wife's belongings remained untouched in the master bedroom, and her own clothes were confined to a hallway cupboard. While Brian justified this as an act of compassion for his children, Ruby felt like an outsider in what was supposed to be their home. Each time she raised her discomfort, Brian dismissed her feelings, framing her requests as trivial or insensitive. Over time, these small dismissals deepened into emotional distance. Ruby's sense of self-worth diminished as she realised that the space she had sacrificed so much to build was still occupied, not by another woman, but by her lingering presence.

Adrian and Mandy's experience unfolded differently, but the outcome was strikingly similar. When Adrian moved into Mandy's home, he brought with him many of his late wife's cherished belongings, wanting to keep her memory close. Mandy suggested keeping only a few sentimental pieces, hoping to create a balance between remembrance and renewal. But Adrian resisted, interpreting her request as disrespectful to his late wife's memory. His inability to part with these items slowly filled their shared spaces with reminders of the past, from furniture to décor, and eventually, a new shrine that included his late wife's ashes. What Mandy had hoped would become their home began to feel like a museum of his former life. The emotional weight of these reminders left her feeling like a guest, not a partner, and ultimately contributed to the breakdown of their five-year relationship.

Across these cases, and in my own experience with Bill, a clear pattern emerges: unhealed grief often leaves widowers struggling to balance loyalty to the past with commitment to the present. When a home, emotionally or physically, remains anchored to the late wife, the new partner can feel invisible, living in the shadow of someone who is no longer there. Over time, this can erode self-esteem, lead to deep emotional fatigue, or foster resentment. I remember countless private moments of feeling torn between understanding his grief and feeling guilty for wanting space in our shared home.

From a psychological perspective, these behaviours often arise from the concept of *continuing bonds theory*, which suggests that maintaining emotional or physical connections to the deceased, through belongings, rituals, or places, helps people to preserve a sense of stability during grief [4]. While these connections can be comforting for the widower, when they dominate the new relationship, they prevent emotional reinvestment in the present.

Experts in grief counselling, such as Dr Robert Neimeyer and James Worden, note that physical reminders can play a powerful role in meaning reconstruction after loss, helping the bereaved sustain identity and continuity. Yet they also warn that overreliance on these objects can trap individuals between two worlds, unable to fully grieve or grow [4][16]. In relationships, this dynamic can also be a red flag because one partner is living in the past while the other struggles to feel seen in the present.

Recognising these red flags isn't about blame; it's about awareness. A widower who keeps his late wife's belongings untouched or resists creating new memories isn't necessarily unkind or selfish; he may be emotionally stuck, navigating grief in a way that protects him from pain. But for the new partner, the emotional toll can be profound. The new partner often bears the emotional weight, continuously negotiating, compromising, and trying to create space in a life that still feels anchored to the past.

Opening the Conversation

When a widower continues to hold on to or display his late wife's belongings, it can stir complex emotions for his new partner, confusion, sadness, and even guilt for wanting space of her own. Starting a conversation about these objects requires sensitivity and courage.

It's not just about furniture, photos, or keepsakes; it's about emotional boundaries, belonging, and finding space for a new story to unfold. These conversations are best approached with compassion rather than confrontation. They open the door to understanding his emotional attachment while also expressing your own need for inclusion and balance.

Start by sharing your feelings using *"I" statements* that express how the situation affects you, without placing blame or criticism. This helps your partner hear your emotions rather than feel defensive.

- "I feel a little out of place when I see so many reminders of your late wife around the house. I'd love for us to find ways to make this space feel like ours."
- "I really value the memories you have with her, but sometimes I struggle to find where I fit into your world."

This approach allows you to be vulnerable while inviting understanding, rather than conflict.

Encouraging your partner to talk about what these items mean to him can help uncover the emotional ties behind them, whether they're a source of comfort, guilt, or lingering grief.

- "What do these items represent for you?"
- "How do you feel when you see or touch these things?"
- "What's hardest about letting go of some of her belongings?"

These kinds of questions aren't about erasing the past; they're about helping him articulate how it still lives within him. Often, this understanding becomes the first step toward emotional clarity.

Suggest creating shared or blended spaces that honour both the past and the present.

- "Would you feel comfortable if we created a small keepsake area just for her things, and then built a new space that reflects both of us?"

- "What if we chose something together, a piece of décor, a trip, or a photo, that symbolises our new chapter?"

This approach helps balance respect for his history with the creation of new shared meaning, a foundation for emotional intimacy and renewal.

Many widowers fear that reducing visible reminders of their late wife is a kind of betrayal. Reassuring him that it's about making room, not replacing love, can help soften that fear.

- "I know how special she was to you. Making space for us doesn't take away from what you shared, it just means there's room for both of us."
- "You'll always have those memories; we're just trying to build some new ones too."

If these discussions become emotionally charged or repetitive, it may be time to step back and evaluate the relationship or consider professional guidance. Grief counselling or couples therapy can offer tools to help both partners communicate with understanding rather than frustration.

What to Remember

Honouring the past and building a future aren't mutually exclusive, but they do require balance, honesty, and compassion. Creating a new life together means making space for each other physically and emotionally, for both partners to feel that they belong.

Chapter 13 – How Past Routines Shape the Present

"I started to wonder if he loved me or just loved that I could step into the life he already had planned with her."

"He wasn't trying to discover new things with me, just trying to recreate what he missed."

This chapter examines why some widowers hope, or even expect, their new partner to share the hobbies, tastes, or routines of their late wife. These expectations usually come from emotional needs: nostalgia, unresolved grief, or simply the comfort of familiar patterns. For the widower, it can feel perfectly natural. For the new partner, though, it can feel like being asked to step into someone else's shoes rather than being valued for who she is. Expectations may be subtle or obvious, but either way, they can spark feelings of displacement or inadequacy. Through real-life examples and personal reflections, this chapter shows how couples have navigated these tricky waters.

In my experience, Bill often encouraged me to join in routines and hobbies he had shared with his late wife. At first, I didn't fully understand what was happening, but over time I began to question whether his request stemmed from an unspoken expectation that I 'fill in' for her. Towards the end of our relationship, I increasingly felt more like a live-in friend or placeholder than a partner building a shared life. Eventually, the subtle pressure to replicate his past left me feeling second-best, emotionally sidelined, and unsure of my place in our relationship.

Professionals such as Dr Susan J. Elliott note that widowers may unconsciously cling to shared routines as a way to keep the late wife's memory alive, which can unintentionally make the new partner feel like a substitute. In my case, Bill didn't initially realise that what comforted him was causing me pain. I longed to create our own routines and experiences, to build a unique bond rather than live in the shadow of his past.

Case Study - Kylie and Alex

Kylie, a middle-aged woman who never had much interest in sports, began dating Alex, a widower whose late wife had been very active and loved going to the gym. As a birthday surprise, Alex bought Kylie a gym membership for the same gym he and his late wife used to attend together. Along with this, he gifted Kylie gym clothes that she felt were revealing, not her type, and better suited to his late wife's figure than Kylie's own body shape. Kylie felt deeply uncomfortable with this gift. It triggered old body image insecurities and anxiety, especially as she is a sexual assault survivor who felt unsafe exercising in an environment full of strangers. Knowing that his late wife had been a self-described gym junkie who proudly wore skimpy workout clothes only intensified Kylie's sense that she was being pushed to fill a role she had never wanted or would put her hand up for. Instead of feeling loved for who she was, Kylie felt as though she was being asked to become someone else. Kylie only used the gym membership to use the toilets, as they were cleaner than the toilets at the nearby car park where she parked almost daily for work.

Case Study- Julie and Nigel

Julie had been dating Nigel for three months when he invited her to a dinner at a restaurant he hadn't visited in over a year. As they were seated, Nigel casually told the server, "We'll have the usual." Julie had never been there before. Nigel explained that he and his late wife, Beth, had gone every Wednesday for more than fifteen years, always ordering the same meals. Soon, the familiar dishes arrived, and the restaurant owner asked after Beth, glancing at Julie with a disapproving look. Nigel explained that Beth had passed away nearly a year earlier. The owner, visibly upset, began reminiscing about Beth at length. Throughout the evening, Nigel made no effort to introduce Julie, leaving her feeling invisible and awkward. When the bill arrived, the owner announced that Nigel's meal and drinks were on the house, leaving only Julie's to be paid for. Without consulting her, Nigel booked a table for two for the following Wednesday. Conversation throughout the night focused almost entirely on memories of Beth. Julie felt like an intruder in someone else's life, as though she were stepping into a role that wasn't hers. What was meant to be a special date left her questioning whether Nigel was truly interested in building a new life with her, or if he was simply clinging to the past.

Case Study – Laura and Stephen

Laura found herself in an uncomfortable position when her partner, Stephen, insisted that all their food shopping must be done at the same shops his late wife had frequented. Stephen reasoned that Laura was new to the area, and his late wife had known best where to shop. At first, Laura tried to adapt to Stephen's routine, but over time, she felt increasingly alienated and unseen in the relationship. Shopping together, which could have been an opportunity to create new shared habits, instead became a painful reminder that she was living in the shadow of another woman's choices. This dynamic left Laura feeling secondary, as though her preferences didn't matter, and she was merely stepping into a role pre-designed by Stephen's late wife. The experience contributed to growing frustration and sadness, as Laura questioned whether there was room for her individuality within their life together.

Recognising the Red Flags

Across these case studies, consistent patterns appear. Unhealed grief can subtly, or sometimes overtly, shape the dynamics of a new relationship. In Kylie's experience, Alex's well-meaning gift of a gym membership and clothes mirrored the lifestyle and choices of his late wife. Instead of feeling loved for who she was, Kylie felt as though she was being asked to fit into a role that wasn't hers, intensifying her insecurities and sense of displacement.

Similarly, Julie and Nigel's dinner at the restaurant shows how routines from a past marriage can create a shadow over new relationships. Nigel's repeated visits, focused conversation, and the server's attention to his late wife left Julie feeling invisible, awkward, and like an intruder in a life that was supposed to be theirs together.

Laura and Stephen's story shows how even small, practical habits, like sticking to stores the late wife preferred, can quietly send the message that the new partner's likes and choices come second. Instead of co-creating shared routines, Laura felt as though she was stepping into a life pre-scripted by someone else, eroding her sense of individuality and belonging.

Professional insight explains why this happens. *Continuing bonds theory* suggests that widowers often maintain physical or behavioural connections to their late spouse as a way to manage grief and sustain a sense of emotional stability [17]. Maintaining routines, revisiting places, or encouraging a new partner to adopt shared hobbies from the past can feel comforting for a widower and serve as a way to preserve identity and continuity and to avoid fully confronting loss

[4][5]. Sometimes, these behaviours aren't conscious at all; they're just a way of holding on to past happiness or guarding against the fear of forgetting a life that once mattered [23].

While these patterns are often unintentional, the emotional impact on the new partner can be profound. Feeling pressured to mirror past routines, step into pre-established roles, or adopt preferences that aren't their own can trigger feelings of invisibility, inadequacy, and emotional exhaustion. Over time, this may erode self-esteem and create tension in the relationship, even if the widower has no conscious intent to harm.

Experts emphasise that recognising the red flags is a matter of awareness. Couples can benefit from openly discussing these patterns and intentionally creating new shared experiences. This allows the widower to honour the past while entirely investing in the present, and ensures that the new partner feels seen, valued, and included in a relationship built on mutual respect and co-created memories [8][23].

Opening the Conversation

When a widower's attachment to routines, hobbies, or belongings from a past marriage begins to overshadow your shared life, gentle, honest communication is key. These conversations are not about blaming or criticising, they are about expressing your experience and creating space for both the past and present to coexist.

"I feel like I'm stepping into routines that don't reflect who I am, and it makes it hard for me to feel fully included in our life together."

"What do these routines or hobbies mean to you?"

"How do you feel when we visit these places?"

"Could we pick a restaurant, hobby, or activity that becomes our own?"

"I understand how important these routines are to you, and I'd like us to find a balance so we both feel comfortable."

By approaching these conversations with interest, kindness, and transparency, you can protect your emotional well-being, honour the widower's grief, set healthy boundaries and foster a partnership that respects both the past and the present.

What to Remember

While it's natural for grieving widowers to hold on to some past routines and traditions, it becomes a problem when these patterns overshadow the new partner or the shared relationship. A healthy partnership honours the past but prioritises the present, ensuring that the life you build together belongs equally to both people.

Chapter 14 - When Jewellery Holds Memories

"I remember looking at the ring he gave me, knowing it belonged to her first, and thinking: Am I building a future on top of someone else's past?"

"When he had her rings melted into something new, it felt creative, but seeing it on his wedding finger every day was like a quiet reminder that part of him still belonged to her."

"It felt like our relationship was haunted by love he never stopped having, and that love was wearing a ring, too."

Jewellery belonging to a widower's late wife often carries deep sentimental value, acting as a tangible connection to past love, memory, and shared life. In some cases, widowers may offer these items to their new partner, or keep them visible, which can create complex emotions for both parties. While the intention is often to honour memory or share connection, for the new partner, being asked to wear or care for these pieces can feel uncomfortable, as if stepping into a role that isn't truly theirs.

From my own experience, Bill gave my daughter his late wife's ruby ring for her birthday, which left me feeling conflicted. He didn't give similar gifts to my other children, only to the one who shared a birthday with his late wife. Moments like this brought forward a lingering sense of being overshadowed by the past.

Bill gave me a necklace that had belonged to his late wife for Christmas during our fifth year together. Although I tried to show gratitude, it was deeply upsetting, and my daughter noticed me fighting back tears. That gift reinforced a sense that I was living in the shadow of his past. We separated a few weeks later, just days before the anniversary of his wedding to his late wife.

Professionals explain this attachment as part of *"continuing bonds,"* where objects can help the widower maintain a sense of connection to the deceased [17]. Jewellery, in particular, can act as a symbolic link to identity, love, and shared experiences. While these items can soothe the widower's grief, they may unintentionally create emotional barriers in his new relationship.

There are practical ways to navigate these situations. Some widowers choose to recreate jewellery into new designs, gift it to family members, store it safely as keepsakes, or even donate pieces to charity. These options honour the late spouse's memory while creating space for the new relationship to grow.

Case Study – Evelyn and Tray

Evelyn and Tray had been together for four years when Tray decided it was time to propose. Wanting everything to be perfect, he planned a romantic weekend away at a beautiful coastal town known for its sunsets and intimate restaurants. Tray also took his late wife's engagement ring to a jeweller to have it cleaned and resized, believing it would add meaning to their commitment.

One evening, over candlelight, Tray got down on one knee. The entire restaurant paused, eyes fixed on them, as Evelyn said her heart raced with joy and anticipation. Then Tray opened the box and, with a loving smile, slipped the ring onto her finger.

In that instant, Evelyn's joy collided with an unexpected ache. She immediately recognised the ring as belonging to Tray's late wife, a piece she had seen in photos displayed in their home. Tears sprang to her eyes, but they weren't purely happy tears. She felt torn: deeply in love with Tray and wanting to say yes, yet unsettled by wearing something so entwined with another woman's memory.

In the moment, she told Tray her tears were from happiness, unsure how to express the heaviness in her heart without spoiling what he clearly intended as a romantic gesture. Tray never mentioned his late wife that night; instead, he focused on celebrating them, toasting to the future. Yet for Evelyn, the unspoken presence of his past relationship hovered silently over their evening.

Later, back at the hotel, Evelyn found Tray's final surprise, a beautiful bouquet of flowers. Though touched by his effort, she still felt a quiet sadness she couldn't fully share.

When they returned home, Evelyn struggled to show the ring to family and friends. Each glance at her hand reminded her of Tray's life before her, and she silently questioned why he chose this ring rather than creating something new for *them*. Wearing it made her feel both loved and like she was living in someone else's story, a conflict she carried alone.

Case study – Fiona and Callum

Fiona and Callum had been together for nearly eighteen months when Callum made a choice that quietly unsettled her. Without consulting Fiona, he took several of his late wife's rings, including her engagement ring and both their wedding bands, to a jeweller. There, he had them melted down and remade into a single new ring, which he chose to wear on his wedding finger.

When he first showed her the finished piece, Fiona was polite and supportive on the surface. After all, he was no longer wearing his wedding ring, which he had stopped using months after they met. Yet beneath the surface, she felt an unexpected sadness and unease she couldn't quite name every time she looked at it.

Seeking clarity, Fiona spoke to her counsellor, hoping to untangle her feelings. But the response she received, "Oh, how lovely!" and "What a wonderful way to reuse jewellery that wasn't going to be worn", left her feeling more self-doubting. She wondered if she was being unreasonable or selfish.

Privately, Fiona wrestled with questions she couldn't voice aloud. Why hadn't Callum chosen to pass these rings to his three adult daughters or his son? Why remake them for himself rather than creating a keepsake for the family? Fiona wondered if wearing the ring on his wedding finger symbolically linked him to his past marriage instead of leaving space for a possible future one with her.

Fiona kept reminding herself that his new ring didn't even resemble the originals. Yet she couldn't shake the quiet presence of his late wife that seemed woven into their relationship through this single piece of jewellery. She tried to suppress her doubts, determined to be reasonable and supportive, but every time the ring caught the light on his hand, she silently asked herself what it might mean for their future together.

Recognising the Red Flags

Both case studies reveal striking emotional parallels. Tray proposed with his late wife's engagement ring, presenting it directly to Evelyn as a symbol of their future together. Callum had his late wife's rings, including her wedding bands, melted into a new ring, which he then wore himself.

For both Evelyn and Fiona, the gestures stirred a lot of inner conflict. Evelyn's joy was immediately shadowed by grief and confusion. She wanted to marry Tray, but the ring still felt like it belonged to someone else. Fiona was unsettled by Callum's choice, hurt, and struggled to put her feelings into words, later questioning whether she was being selfish or unreasonable. Both women carried guilt, shame, and self-doubt over what outsiders might see as "just jewellery," but for them, the emotional weight was very real. Their discomfort was made worse by silence or dismissive responses: Evelyn couldn't speak up in the moment, hiding her tears behind a smile, and Fiona's conversation with a counsellor only made her doubt herself further. These stories show how unspoken or minimised feelings can leave a new partner feeling invisible, sidelined, or completely isolated.

Research into grief, attachment, and continuing bonds helps explain why these situations hit so hard. Grief expert J. William Worden notes that keeping, repurposing, or wearing items like rings and jewellery is often part of a widower's continuing bond—a way to hold on to the deceased, offering comfort and a sense of ongoing connection. These bonds to pieces of jewellery aren't meant to hurt a new partner, but when they take centre stage or aren't discussed, they can unintentionally overshadow the present relationship, leaving the new partner feeling excluded, in emotional competition, or displaced [8] [22].

A widower might not always realise just how much keeping or cherishing his late wife's jewellery can mean, or how it lands for his new partner. For some, refashioning pieces or keeping them on display is simply a way to honour the life they shared, not a comment on the current relationship.

The difference usually comes down to communication. When a widower openly involves his partner, acknowledges that certain items might cause discomfort, and works together on how to honour the past while prioritising the present, the emotional impact is far gentler. These conversations let both people feel seen and respected, balance remembrance with the needs of the relationship, build trust, and protect emotional safety.

Opening the Conversation

If offered jewellery feels uncomfortable, it's possible to decline politely while showing respect for the widower's grief. For example:

- "Thank you for thinking of me; it means a lot. I feel this piece belongs to your family and her memory, and I'd rather honour that."
- "I appreciate your kindness, but I'd feel more comfortable if this jewellery stayed within your family as part of her legacy."

Saying no does not reject the relationship or disrespect the memory of the late wife; it simply protects your own comfort and sense of self. Sometimes, widowers extend these gestures to the new partner's family. While intended to foster inclusion, this can feel emotionally complicated, especially when the items hold deep sentimental value. Honest, compassionate conversation is key:

- "I'm grateful you wanted to include my family, but I feel these pieces should remain part of your family's history and memory."
- "It's thoughtful, but my daughter doesn't feel comfortable wearing something so special that belonged to someone she never knew."

The goal is to find ways to honour the past without overshadowing the present, and to establish boundaries that safeguard emotional well-being for everyone involved.

By understanding the symbolic meaning of jewellery, acknowledging personal discomfort, and approaching the topic with kindness and clarity, couples can navigate these delicate issues. This allows the new relationship to flourish while still respecting the memory of the person who came before.

What to Remember

While keeping or repurposing a late wife's jewellery can help a widower maintain a comforting bond, it may unintentionally place the new partner in the shadow of the past, making her feel like a second choice or a replacement.

Chapter 15 - The Shrine

"I was relieved when he scattered her ashes and removed the shrine."

"I wish he'd asked how I felt instead of assuming I'd be okay with it."

"I didn't like the fact that the living area had the remains of a dead person in it."

"Part of me understood why he kept the shrine, but part of me felt like I'd never measure up."

A shrine is a space set aside to remember someone who has died. For many widowers, creating one for their late wife is deeply meaningful, a way to stay connected and ritualise grief. These spaces might include ashes, framed photos, personal keepsakes, favourite ornaments, or any objects carrying emotional weight. In some cultures, home altars or shrines are a normal part of mourning or ancestor remembrance, with candles, religious symbols, or treasured items helping keep memories alive.

While shrines can bring comfort and help process loss, they can also affect a new partner's sense of belonging and emotional safety. Seeing a shrine in shared living spaces can be a constant reminder that the widower's heart is still tied to the past. Even if unintentional, it can send the message that the deceased holds a central place in the home—and in his life.

In my own experience, Bill had created a shrine to his late wife on the coffee table in our living room. At the centre of the arrangement were her ashes, surrounded by her favourite personal items and keepsakes. At first, I didn't fully grasp the significance of the objects neatly placed on the table. When I realised that a seemingly decorative candle holder was actually an urn, and that every surrounding item belonged to his late wife, the reality of the shrine hit me. I remember thinking, "It's a living room, not a cemetery," and immediately feeling guilty for thinking it. I also felt creeped out, especially when I remembered that we had kissed and been intimate in front of the shrine, completely unaware of its true significance at the time. The experience left me conflicted, trying to honour his grief while also navigating my own discomfort and need for a home that reflected both of us.

Case Study - Hannah and Michael

Hannah moved in with Michael two years after they met. Michael had a glass cabinet in the living room displaying his late wife's ashes, wedding ring, and photos from their life together. At first, Hannah respected his need to remember his late wife, but over time, she found it painful and a source of discomfort as the shrine prompted questions and conversations relating to Michael's late wife from friends and family. Hannah found it difficult to know what to do when she dusted. She didn't want to dust the shrine, but at the same time, she felt it would be odd to dust everything else in the room and leave the shrine untouched.

When Hannah gently raised her worries with Michael, he became defensive and insisted that changing the shrine would be a betrayal of his late wife's memory. Hannah struggled with guilt for wanting change, but also felt hurt that Michael didn't acknowledge her discomfort.

Case Study - Lisa and Andrew

Lisa and Andrew began dating three years after Andrew's wife passed away. Andrew kept a small shelf in his study with framed photos of his late wife, including their favourite wedding photo, their wedding rings, and a pendant that he once tried to gift to Lisa. The space was private, and Andrew openly shared its meaning with Lisa, explaining that it helped him feel gratitude rather than sadness.

Lisa appreciated Andrew's honesty, but she still felt confused and wondered if he was still grieving. Lisa asked Andrew if his late wife had to look at photos of his ex-wife, the woman he loved before her? Andrew became defensive and snapped at Lisa, saying, "This is different, my ex-wife is still alive, and my late wife would not make me feel bad for having a shrine".

Andrew felt that Lisa had become demanding and was being insensitive to his needs. Andrew was so upset that he went to the cemetery to sit by his late wife's grave. Lisa tried to communicate her discomfort and her questions about Andrew's shrine to his late wife and found herself with more questions than answers.

Lisa felt unseen and unheard. The shrine grew larger in her mind each day. She decided to call off her relationship with Andrew the day she found him drunk and curled up on his study floor, hugging his late wife's wedding dress, and surrounded by photos and items that belonged to his late wife. Lisa asked him if he was okay, and he swore at Lisa and then accused her of being jealous of his late wife.

Recognising the Red Flags

Both Hannah and Lisa entered relationships where their partners maintained physical reminders of their late wives, reflecting what the grief researchers call *continuing bonds* [17]. At first, a shrine may symbolise love and remembrance, but over time, it can become an emotional barrier that quietly shapes the dynamics of their relationships.

For Hannah, Michael's glass cabinet, displaying his late wife's ashes, wedding ring, and photos, dominated the living room. It made her feel as though she was sharing her home and his emotional space with someone she could never replace. Lisa's experience with Andrew was different in form but similar in impact. His private shrine, tucked away in his study yet emotionally charged, created a world she could never fully enter.

Both women approached their partners' grief with empathy, yet when they expressed discomfort, their concerns were met with defensiveness rather than understanding.

Red flags can include:

- Shrines or memorials that dominate shared living spaces

- Defensiveness or anger when the new partner expresses discomfort or asks questions about the shrine.
- Emotional withdrawal or prioritising grief over the current relationship.
- Lack of communication about how past memories coexist with the present.
- Feeling unseen, invisible, or like a "second choice" in the home.

These patterns often leave the new partner feeling sidelined and unsure of her place in the relationship. Even when grounded in genuine grief, such dynamics can quietly overshadow the present, making it difficult for the couple to build a shared life.

From a professional perspective, psychologists explain that maintaining a shrine or other physical reminders of their late wife can echo the *continuing bonds* theory: widowers preserve objects and spaces to sustain an ongoing emotional connection with the deceased, integrating their loss into daily life [17]. These objects can offer comfort, reinforce identity, and represent loyalty, helping the widower navigate unresolved grief.

However, experts caution that when these bonds are unspoken, dominate shared spaces, or are maintained without dialogue, they can unintentionally create emotional distance within the new relationship [4][22]. Attachment theory suggests that unresolved loss can disrupt a person's ability to form secure new bonds, leaving partners at risk of feeling secondary or excluded [29]. Hannah's experience fits into Pauline Boss's concept of *ambiguous loss*, living with someone who is physically present but emotionally absent [9]. Lisa's experience, marked by defensiveness and anger, illustrates how unprocessed grief can surface as emotional control or withdrawal, escalating tension when the new partner raises valid concerns.

Professional insight underscores the importance of open communication and clear boundaries. Dr Susan J. Elliott and other grief experts emphasise that discussing the meaning of memorial items, agreeing on how they're displayed, and creating new rituals together can help honour the past while making room for the present [8]. Red flags can often be managed when addressed openly: widowers who involve their partners, acknowledge potential discomfort, and collaborate on balancing remembrance with shared life allow both individuals to feel respected, valued, and emotionally safe [22].

Opening the Conversation

When a widower maintains a shrine or memorial to his late wife, opening a conversation about it can feel daunting. Many women worry they will appear insensitive, jealous, or dismissive of grief. Gentle but honest conversations can help bring unspoken discomfort into the open and create space for mutual understanding.

When discussing the shrine with your partner, the aim is to remain calm, respectful, and grounded in your own emotional experience rather than criticism. These conversation starters offer simple, compassionate ways to open the discussion:

• "I want to talk about something that's been sitting with me. I respect your connection to your late wife, but I'm finding it hard to feel at home with the shrine in our shared space."

• "I'm not asking you to let go of your past. I do need to understand how we can make room for both of us in this home."

• "I've noticed I feel uneasy and unsure of my place when I see the shrine. I'd like to talk about what it means to you and share how it affects me."

• "I want us to build a shared life together. Can we talk about how remembrance and our relationship can coexist in a way that feels safe for us both?"

• "I'm struggling to find my footing emotionally, and I don't want that to turn into resentment. I'd rather talk about it openly now."

If the shrine is located in a shared living area, it may also help to explore practical boundaries together:

> • "Would you be open to talking about where the shrine lives in the house, so our shared spaces feel like they belong to both of us?"

> • "Is there a way we could honour her memory while also creating areas that reflect our relationship?"

Opening these conversations can feel uncomfortable, especially when grief, loyalty, and fear of conflict are involved. A receptive response, one that includes listening, reassurance, and a willingness to reflect, often signals emotional availability. Defensiveness, anger, or refusal to acknowledge discomfort may indicate that grief is still dominating the emotional space of the relationship.

Speaking up is not a rejection of the past. It is an invitation to bring honesty into the present. Whether the conversation leads to compromise, deeper understanding, or clarity about what the relationship can offer, giving voice to your feelings restores agency and affirms your right to feel safe, seen, and at home.

What to Remember

A shrine can honour love that shaped the widower's life, but it can also create invisible walls around the heart. Open conversation and compassionate boundaries can help transform memory from a barrier into a bridge toward a shared future. A shrine may also be a sign that the widower is not ready to give his heart to another woman.

Dear Me

I didn't realise how deeply this would affect me. I thought I was stepping into a relationship where we'd build something new, a future, a connection, a love that could stand on its own. But instead, I slowly found myself standing in the shadow of someone who had already lived the love story I never got to be part of.

I tried to be understanding. I told myself this was grief, and grief is complicated. I gave space. I stayed quiet when memories flooded in on anniversaries, through social media reminders, in the stories he told to anyone who'd listen, stories that rarely included me. But over time, I began to feel like I was in the wrong room, like I'd entered halfway through a play where the lead actress had already taken her final bow, and I was just an understudy waiting behind the curtain.

There were moments I questioned whether I was being overly sensitive. But then I'd find myself surrounded by her belongings, hearing *"we"* and *"us"* when he meant *him and her,* and I'd realise again I was never really invited into this story.

Worse, there were times I knew deep down that the marriage he mourned wasn't as perfect as he claimed, as he often spoke of tension, of emotional distance, even regret. But those wounds still lived in him, and sometimes, they were passed onto me. I became the new partner bearing the weight of old pain.

So, here's what I know now: Grief is real. Love is real. But sometimes, they're not enough to build something sustainable, not if only one is trying to make room for both the past and the present. If the relationship isn't strong enough to carry us both, then I have permission to set it down gently.

I don't feel guilty for choosing myself. If I ache, I'll let myself grieve not just for what we had, but for what never really got the chance to be. I know now that I'm not here to compete with memory. I'm here to live, love, and be loved fully, equally, *now*.

And I promise myself this: I will not dim my light to fit into someone else's mourning. I will no longer play a part in a story that doesn't have room for *me*.

With love. **Me**

Part 3 – Friends and Relations

My adult children welcomed Bill with genuine warmth from the very beginning. They opened their hearts to him and embraced the idea that I had found love again. Bill often spoke about his late wife with my friends and family; though none of them had ever met her, they soon knew many details of her life.

It wasn't until after our separation that I learned he would wait until I left the room to reminisce about her. He had told some of my closest people that I disapproved of him speaking about his late wife, a comment that could have made me seem cold or unsupportive. Those who truly know me understand that isn't who I am.

That revelation was deeply painful. Looking back, I remember moments when I re-entered a room and sensed an uneasy silence, the kind that tells you you've just interrupted a conversation you weren't meant to hear. Now I understand why.

My grandchildren adored Bill and affectionately called him "Pop Bill." At the time, it felt like a natural, beautiful connection, a sign of love expanding to include him. But after our relationship ended, I regretted encouraging that bond. The children were hurt, and I felt their pain when he withdrew completely, retreating back into the world he'd once shared with his late wife. Almost immediately, he began wearing her ashes again in the locket around his neck, something he hadn't worn for years. It felt as though our time together, and everyone connected to it, had been quickly erased.

Bill and his late wife didn't have children, so I can't speak from personal experience about blending families with widowers who do. Yet through countless conversations with women who have loved widowers, a clear pattern emerges: when children are involved, particularly without firm boundaries or emotional clarity, they can unintentionally shape, strain, or even undermine the new relationship.

For some children (young and old), it's difficult to see their father with someone new, even many years after their mother's death. But the tension can be especially volatile when the loss is still fresh.

There's also the extended network, the late wife's family, friends, and social circles that often remain tightly woven into the widower's life. Club members or community groups where she once played a central role may quietly, or sometimes quite openly, resist welcoming someone new. Many women I've spoken with have described the unmistakable signs of exclusion: the half-finished introductions, the sideways glances, the pointed corrections when they're referred to not by name, but simply as "the new woman." You're never quite her, and they never quite let you forget it.

Then there are the well-meaning people in the widower's life who encourage you to take on the role the late wife once held. They might suggest that you cook her favourite recipes, follow her traditions, or even use her belongings. Others, often her closest friends, seem to go out of their way to interfere. They remind him of who she was. They ask if he remembers that holiday, that song, that birthday surprise, as if you're a temporary placeholder until his real past returns.

It's important to acknowledge the cultural and emotional pressure placed on new partners to become an audience for the widower's grief. Family and friends often expect you to listen to endless stories from the past, even when those stories come at the cost of your own voice, presence, and emotional space. You're expected to honour her memory while trying to build a future with the man you love.

But here's the truth: I've come to understand you cannot build a shared life with someone who is still living in a life already shared. There's a difference between remembering and remaining. Between grief and loyalty. Between love and emotional unavailability. And for anyone loving a widower, you deserve to be seen, not just tolerated. You deserve to be honoured in the present, not merely asked to honour the past.

In those cases, the widower may be seeking comfort, companionship, or simply relief from aching loneliness. While that may seem gentle or unintentional, it often places the new partner in a role they never chose, a source of comfort rather than a genuine partner in a relationship founded on mutual emotional readiness and equality.

Chapter 16 - When They Become Protectors of the Past

"I felt like a guest in my own home."

"Every time his daughter changed something back 'the way Mum had it,' it felt like she was erasing me from his life."

"Sometimes I felt like I was in a relationship with three other people: my fiancé, his adult daughter, and his late wife"

In this chapter, we explore how some new partners can face resistance from a widower's children, most commonly daughters, who, driven by loyalty and unresolved grief, step into the role of guardians of their late mother's memory. Occasionally, a son may display similar protective behaviours. These children can unconsciously sabotage their father's new relationship in an effort to preserve the emotional status quo in the family. Their protectiveness is rarely deliberate; it is often grounded in fear of loss, devotion to their mother, and the belief that welcoming someone new somehow diminishes the past.

As the family system shifts, some daughters struggle to adapt. They may question the new partner's intentions, closely monitor interactions, or offer unsolicited opinions about the relationship. In some cases, the widower enables this behaviour by granting his child an unhealthy level of influence over his decisions, where to go, what to celebrate, who attends family events, and even when it is appropriate to express affection toward the new partner. When boundaries are weak, emotional enmeshment can occur, blurring roles and reinforcing the child's belief that they have a right to protect their mother's memory and shield their father from change.

Unresolved grief can cause family members to cling tightly to symbols of the past, resisting new emotional attachments as a way of preserving what once was. For some daughters, this often results in policing access to their father, holding emotional power within the household, and subtly keeping the new partner on the outside.

When a widower does not establish clear boundaries, the message, intended or not, is that his child's feelings come first, while the new partner's emotional needs are secondary. Over time, this dynamic can erode trust, create tension, and leave the new partner feeling as though they are competing not only with a memory but with the living embodiment of it.

Recognising this pattern does not place blame on daughters, sons, or widowers. Rather, it highlights how grief can reshape family roles in ways that appear protective but are ultimately damaging. Healthy relationships require clear boundaries, emotional space, and the willingness to allow new bonds to grow, without expecting anyone to disappear.

Case Study – Kylie

Kylie has been living with her fiancé, Peter, for six months, and they have been together for two years.

Peter's adult daughter frequently lets herself into their home unannounced, rearranges the kitchen to match how it had been during her mother's life, goes through Peter's mail while discarding Kylie's, and calls him for hours each day. She also organised lunch dates that excluded Kylie and hung new photos of her late mother on the walls. These repeated intrusions and exclusions left Kylie feeling invisible, undermined, and emotionally exhausted.

When Kylie raised her concerns with Peter, he tried to intervene, asking his daughter to respect boundaries and stop discarding Kylie's mail. However, his daughter dismissed Kylie's concerns as lies, portrayed her as a troublemaker, and pressured Peter to end the relationship.

Case Study – Kate and Robert

Kate entered her marriage to Robert believing they could build a new life together in the home they had purchased. However, Robert's twenty-year-old daughter resisted Kate's presence from the beginning. She ignored Kate's authority, showed open hostility toward Kate's children, and insisted that only she truly understood her father. She demanded that her parents' wedding photo remain beside Robert and Kate's, as if the past and present marriages should share the same space.

Roberts' daughter also disregarded her new baby half-brother and manipulated situations to keep control of her father's attention, often interrupting scarce date nights by pretending to be sick or in danger. The constant hostility, emotional manipulation, and refusal to accept the new family dynamic left Kate emotionally depleted. She began to worry about Robert's daughter's mental health and unresolved grief, while also questioning the future of her marriage.

Case Study – Linda and Gregory

Linda and Gregory had been together for three years and engaged for two and a half. Gregory's late wife had passed away five years earlier, leaving behind three adult daughters who remained closely involved in his daily life.

From the beginning, Linda admired Gregory's dedication to his daughters. However, over time, she began to notice a pattern that made her increasingly uncomfortable. Two of the daughters maintained constant contact with Gregory, sending multiple messages a day to check in on him, often questioning his plans and decisions. If Gregory made arrangements without informing them, such as booking a holiday or making dinner reservations with Linda, they would become upset or withdrawn.

Their involvement extended beyond conversation. The daughters frequently made unsolicited decisions that affected Linda and Gregory's shared life, including rearranging parts of their home and purchasing personal items for Gregory, such as his underwear and deodorant. Their behaviour blurred appropriate boundaries between parent and adult child, leaving Linda feeling excluded and undermined.

The most distressing incident occurred during what was meant to be Linda and Gregory's anniversary weekend. One of Gregory's daughters had organised a surprise Airbnb booking for her father and insisted that he attend. When Gregory and Linda arrived, the daughter appeared disappointed that Linda had joined him. Soon after, the other two daughters arrived, turning what was meant to be a private, romantic celebration into a family gathering centred entirely around Gregory's late wife.

Throughout the weekend, the daughters reminisced about their mother, bringing along photos, funeral memorabilia, and keepsakes to share with their father. When Gregory gently suggested having dinner with Linda to mark their anniversary, one of the daughters became upset, accusing Linda of "trying to manipulate her dad."

Linda described feeling deeply uncomfortable and disrespected. Despite her efforts to be kind and welcoming, Gregory's daughters remained cold and distant. Their behaviour suggested an emotional loyalty to their late mother that overshadowed any acceptance of Gregory's new relationship.

Tensions escalated when the daughters insisted that Gregory draft and sign a prenuptial agreement before the wedding. Their demand implied suspicion toward Linda's intentions, even though she was financially independent and considerably more secure than Gregory.

While Gregory acknowledged that his daughters' behaviour was problematic, he struggled to set firm boundaries. He avoided confrontation out of fear of upsetting them, which left Linda feeling unsupported and invisible. His reluctance to address their overinvolvement allowed the emotional enmeshment to continue unchecked, reinforcing the daughters' control and keeping Gregory tied to the past.

Recognising the Red Flags

Kylie, Kate, and Linda's experiences reveal a recurring dynamic in relationships with widowers: a daughter, or occasionally a son, can consciously or unconsciously, become the guardian of their late mother's memory, placing the past above the present. While each story differs in detail, the underlying patterns are strikingly similar. The new partner often finds herself competing not with a person, but with a family system still entwined in grief, loyalty, and unresolved emotions.

In Kylie's case, control manifested subtly: her fiancé's daughter frequently let herself into their home, rearranged cupboards, discarded Kylie's mail, and decorated the walls with photos of her late mother. Kate experienced more overt resistance: her stepdaughter actively challenged her presence, undermined her authority, and manipulated situations to monopolise her father's attention. Linda's situation illustrated deep emotional enmeshment, with her partner's daughters maintaining constant involvement in his life, questioning decisions, intruding on private plans, and even turning a couple's anniversary weekend into a memorial for their late mother. Across all three cases, the new partners felt invisible, undermined, and like placeholders rather than fully acknowledged participants in the relationship.

Several red flags emerge from these stories. These include repeated intrusions into the home, open hostility or defiance, constant monitoring or interference in couple decisions, exclusion from social or family events, and a widower's failure to establish clear boundaries. When the deceased parent's memory consistently dominates the family system, the new partner may feel sidelined, emotionally drained, or unwelcome.

Family systems and grief psychology help explain why these dynamics occur. Adult children may struggle to accept a new partner due to unresolved grief, loyalty conflicts, and fear of losing their emotional connection to the deceased parent [9]. They cling to familiar roles, routines, and memories as a way to preserve identity, belonging, and emotional continuity within the family system [8].

This dynamic can escalate into emotional enmeshment, where boundaries between family members are blurred. Widowers, seeking comfort or fearing further emotional loss, may unintentionally elevate a child into a role that straddles caregiver, confidant, and gatekeeper [8]. Over time, the child may feel entitled to comment on, interfere with, or control aspects of the new relationship.

Widowers often enable this behaviour for several reasons. They might be avoiding conflict, fearing that challenging a grieving child will cause pain or instability [9]. They may also feel anxious about further loss, seeking the familiar presence of the child as a link to the past. Comfort in routine and parental guilt can reinforce the tendency to prioritise the child's feelings over those of the new partner [8].

Adult children's protective instincts may present as monitoring interactions, issuing unsolicited critiques, or influencing decisions [9]. While often grounded in loyalty and love, these behaviours can subtly assert emotional control, keeping the widower anchored in the past and obstructing the formation of secure, healthy attachments in the present. Recognising these red flags can allow a new partner to identify when grief is reshaping family roles in ways that may undermine their emotional safety, highlighting the need for boundaries, communication, and a conscious effort to prioritise the present alongside remembrance of the past [8][9].

Opening the Conversation

When addressing a widower's children overstepping boundaries or becoming too involved in decisions, empathy and clarity are essential. Focus on your own feelings rather than assigning blame. For example, you might say, "I feel uncomfortable when the kitchen is rearranged without asking," instead of, "Your daughter shouldn't do that." Using personal "I" statements communicates your experience without provoking defensiveness, increasing the chance of a positive outcome.

Professionals recommend having these conversations in a calm, private setting, free from interruptions. Reflective questions can help both partners explore perspectives and expectations, such as:

- "How do you see your daughter's role in our shared home?"
- "What do you feel is fair in terms of her involvement in decisions?"
- "How can we both feel respected and secure in our relationship?"

Women who have faced similar challenges suggest:

- Clearly expressing your emotional needs, emphasising why privacy, mutual respect, and shared decision-making matter.
- Asking how he envisions boundaries with his children and exploring what feels reasonable for both of you.
- Collaboratively agreeing on practical limits, such as restricting unscheduled visits, defining private

areas, or setting expectations for communication.

- Checking in periodically to reassess boundaries as circumstances evolve.

It's important to recognise that, ultimately, it is the widower's responsibility to establish and maintain clear boundaries within their family. Children, especially adult children, may push, test, or resist limits. If the widower is unwilling or unable to assert boundaries, the new partner will continue to feel sidelined, invisible, or undervalued. Professionals note that when the parent does not take this lead, the family system remains anchored in the past, making it difficult for a new relationship to flourish [8][9].

Open, compassionate communication helps balance loyalty to the past with the needs of the present relationship. But if repeated discussions fail to produce change, it may indicate that the widower is not yet emotionally prepared to navigate the complexities of introducing new bonds alongside existing attachments. Recognising this early can prevent prolonged frustration and guide decisions about the relationship's future.

What to Remember

When a widower's child assumes the role of guardian over a late parent's memory, it can quietly undermine the new partner and strain the relationship. Clear boundaries set by the widower are essential to prevent emotional enmeshment and ensure the present relationship is not overshadowed by the past.

Chapter 17 - Children, Loyalty, and Blended Hearts

"They refused to acknowledge me and threw tantrums because I was invited to Christmas".

"His late wife's family would say awful things about me to his children, telling them that I was trying to take their father away from them".

"On our wedding day, his children refused to go along with the plans, making my husband one hour late, and then his eldest destroyed our wedding cake by trying to take the bride figurine off the top".

When a widower with young children enters a new relationship, the challenges can be profound. Children's grief, loyalty to their deceased mother, and struggles to adjust may complicate the new partner's efforts to build a harmonious family life. The new partner often feels caught between wanting to support the children and needing space to establish her own role and identity within the family. At the same time, widowers may unconsciously prioritise their children's attachment to the past, leaving the new partner feeling excluded or like an outsider in her own home.

Family therapists and grief counsellors emphasise the importance of setting clear boundaries, fostering open dialogue, and helping children accept the new partner without feeling disloyal to their late mother. Professional guidance, including grief counselling for children, can be invaluable. Counselling helps children process feelings of loss, loyalty conflicts, and fear of change in a safe environment. It equips them with coping strategies and reduces the likelihood that unresolved grief will be projected onto the new partner, while helping them form healthy attachments and participate in the blended family.

This chapter explores how these dynamics can unfold, drawing on real-life stories and professional insights from family therapists and grief counsellors. Together, they reveal the delicate balance between honouring the past and creating a new, emotionally safe future for everyone involved.

Case Study - Melissa and Matthew

Melissa married Matthew after four years of dating, but his two young children struggled to accept her. Behind Matthew's back, they often behaved rudely, rolling their eyes, ignoring her questions, and whispering insults. More concerningly, they bullied Melissa's younger children, making them feel unsafe in their own home.

Melissa's children eventually told her they wanted to live with their biological father in another state to escape the toxic atmosphere. She felt torn between protecting her children and supporting Matthew's grieving family. The ongoing disrespect left her feeling anxious, helpless, and fearful of losing her own children's trust.

Matthew struggled to believe his children could act this way, as he had never witnessed their behaviour directly. Over time, the emotional strain revealed to

Melissa how unresolved grief and divided loyalties can destabilise a blended family. Ultimately, she realised that love could not survive in a home shadowed by grief and hostility. Melissa ended the relationship before losing herself or her children in the confusion.

Case Study - Olivia and Mark

Olivia and Mark had been together for two years when Mark proposed. Until that point, Mark's children had been friendly and warm toward Olivia, but the engagement changed everything. The children began telling Mark that Olivia treated them unkindly when he wasn't around. Shocked and hurt, Olivia was devastated when Mark felt the need to "have a talk" with her, despite her love and care for his children.

Olivia, who did not have children of her own, had been excited about creating a family with Mark. But she soon felt uneasy as his children's behaviour shifted. They insisted that portraits of their late mother and her belongings remain exactly as they were, even objecting when Olivia rearranged the kitchen to make it more functional. Mark felt caught between protecting his children's feelings and supporting his fiancée.

The children's behaviour escalated to eye-rolling, sarcastic comments, and silent treatment. They also began making false accusations, painting Olivia as unkind to maintain control of their father's attention. Olivia's growing sense of being undermined and falsely accused led her to question the relationship's future, especially as Mark began to side with his children.

Case Study - Tom and Molly

Tom lost his wife after a long battle with cancer. His three children, deeply attached to their mother, struggled to adjust after her death. When Tom shared his intention to marry his new partner, Molly, after 18 months of dating, the children reacted with distress and fear that she would replace their mother's memory.

The eldest child, aged sixteen, began showing signs of depression and withdrawal, struggling academically and socially. Tom was torn between his desire to build a future with Molly and his responsibility to support his children's fragile emotional state. Molly, meanwhile, felt sadness and guilt; she didn't want to add to the children's pain but longed for acceptance as part of the family. When Tom's children pleaded with him not to marry Molly, he ultimately chose to put their needs first. He decided the children were not yet ready for such a change and ended the relationship. For Molly, his decision was heartbreaking, a reminder that love alone cannot heal a family still deeply immersed in grief.

Case Study - Annie and Paul

Paul's late wife passed away when their children were aged one and three.. A few years later, he met Annie, and they have been together for five years and married for three. As the children grew (now aged nine and eleven), they began calling Annie "Mum," seeing her as their mother figure, having no real memories of their biological mother.

However, Paul's late wife's family continued to anchor the children to the past. They frequently shared emotional stories about the deceased mother and insisted the children attend annual memorial events, which left them confused and upset. Despite Paul's repeated attempts to explain that these gatherings were distressing the children, his requests were ignored.

When Paul finally decided the children should no longer attend, his late wife's family accused Annie of trying to erase their daughter's memory. They spoke negatively about her to the children, saying she could never replace their "real mother," and that they shouldn't be calling her "mum", and stopped inviting Paul to family gatherings. Though deeply saddened, Paul stood by his decision, reassuring Annie that it reflected love for their new family, not disrespect for his late wife. Despite the tension, Paul and Annie found strength in each other. They realised that honouring the past does not have to mean surrendering the present.

Recognising the Red Flags

These case studies reveal both common patterns and important distinctions in how widowers manage the process of blending families. In every example, children reacted to the new partner with varying degrees of hostility, resistance, or emotional withdrawal. These responses often stemmed from grief, loyalty to the deceased parent, and fear of losing their emotional connection to that memory. While such reactions are normal within the grieving process, the widower's response determines whether those tensions are healed or deepened.

A key red flag is when the widower fails to take an active leadership role in integrating the new partner into the family. In Matthew and Melissa's case, Matthew did not address his children's bullying or undermining behaviour, leaving Melissa isolated and unsupported. Similarly, Mark often sided with his children over Olivia, and Tom allowed his children's objections to dictate the continuation of his relationship with Molly. Each scenario shows how the absence of clear boundaries, reassurance, or support signals a prioritisation of the past over the present partnership.

By contrast, Paul demonstrated strong emotional leadership. He protected Anne's role within the family by setting firm boundaries with his late wife's relatives, advocating for his children's emotional well-being while affirming Anne's rightful place as their stepmother. His decisiveness allowed the family to acknowledge grief while building a stable and balanced household dynamic.

Professional insight supports these observations. Grief counsellors and family systems experts emphasise that children may project unresolved grief or test loyalty through resistance, sometimes unconsciously [4][8]. A widower who avoids addressing these behaviours often reinforces them, teaching children that emotional control or exclusion is acceptable. Experts agree that widowers must acknowledge their children's pain while also protecting the integrity of the new relationship. Clear, consistent support for the partner, combined with open, age-appropriate dialogue, helps children adjust while validating everyone's emotional needs.

Research also shows that unresolved grief in children can manifest as control, hostility, or resentment toward the new partner, who is perceived as a "replacement" for the late parent [4]. These behaviours can cause deep emotional strain and self-doubt for the new partner while placing the widower in a position of divided loyalty [8]. When he does not set boundaries, the new partner is left to navigate exclusion and conflict alone, creating an emotional imbalance that can undermine the relationship entirely.

Counselling can play a crucial role in addressing these dynamics. Professional support offers children a safe environment to express grief, develop coping strategies, and understand the changes in family structure. It can also help the widower explore his own fears, of loss, guilt, or upsetting his children, that may prevent him from establishing healthy boundaries. When a widower seeks professional guidance, he demonstrates both empathy and strength, showing that grief and new love can coexist without competition.

Ultimately, a widower's leadership is the foundation for successful family blending. Setting boundaries, maintaining open communication, and ensuring emotional safety for both his children and partner are not signs of coldness; they are acts of love and maturity. On the other hand, when leadership is absent, unresolved grief can dominate the household, leaving everyone trapped between the past and the present.

Recognising these red flags is not about placing blame on widowers or children but about understanding how grief can reshape family dynamics in ways that appear protective yet become destructive over time. With empathy, structure, and professional intervention when needed, families can honour the past while still making room for the living present.

Opening the Conversation

Discussing the behaviour of a widower's children or family requires sensitivity, patience, and courage.

These conversations often touch on the deepest parts of grief, loyalty, love, guilt, and fear of loss, and can easily trigger defensiveness if not approached with care. Yet avoiding them allows tension to grow. Speaking honestly and empathetically is the first step toward creating a relationship built on mutual understanding and respect.

Choose a calm, private moment when neither of you feels rushed or emotionally charged. Avoid beginning the discussion in the middle of a conflict or after a difficult interaction with the children. Professionals in grief counselling and family therapy recommend starting from a place of curiosity rather than accusation, seeking to understand, not to win [4][8].

A gentle opening might sound like:

- "I know your children mean a great deal to you, and I want to understand how we can all feel comfortable together."

- "I feel unsettled when I'm excluded from family plans, and I'd like us to talk about how we can find a balance that works for everyone."

Framing the issue around *how you feel* rather than *what someone did* helps to lower defensiveness and invite empathy.

Use *I-statements* to express your experience, *"I feel hurt when I'm not included in decisions about our home"*, rather than *"Your children are shutting me out."*
This language centres the conversation on your emotional needs instead of blaming his children or his parenting choices. It signals that you want collaboration, not confrontation.

Once the conversation begins, invite shared reflection instead of issuing demands. Thoughtful questions can help uncover his perspective and encourage joint problem-solving:

- "What role do you see your children having in our shared life?"

- "How can we make sure both your children and I feel respected?"

- "What boundaries feel fair and realistic for everyone?"

If the children are young, discussions might include agreeing on household routines, shared family activities, or times reserved for the couple alone. For older children, boundaries could involve privacy, respect for personal space, or limits around decision-making in the couple's relationship.

According to family-systems experts, sustainable change depends largely on the widower's willingness to set and maintain boundaries [4][8]. His actions, or inaction, send powerful signals to both his children and his partner. When he establishes clear expectations and consistently supports his partner's role, children learn that love for a new partner does not diminish love for their late mother. Without this leadership, emotional alliances can remain divided, keeping the family stuck in grief and conflict.

Encourage open dialogue about how he envisions balancing loyalty to his children with commitment to his partner. Statements such as *"I know this is difficult for you, and I want to find a way that honours both your children and our relationship"* can help him see boundary-setting as an act of love rather than betrayal.

If discussions repeatedly end in avoidance or defensiveness, it may indicate that grief remains unprocessed or boundaries are too fragile to support a blended relationship. In such cases, professional guidance through counselling or family therapy can help create structure and safety for everyone involved. A therapist can assist the widower in recognising patterns of loyalty conflict and help the couple develop communication strategies that protect both the relationship and the children's well-being.

What to Remember

Healthy communication about children and boundaries is not about choosing sides; it is about creating emotional safety for all. A widower who is willing to listen, lead with empathy, and take responsibility for establishing boundaries demonstrates readiness for a balanced, mature partnership. If those conversations cannot happen or result in ongoing dismissal, it may be a sign that the relationship is still living in the shadow of grief rather than the light of new beginnings.

Chapter 18 - Grief, Grown Children, and the Challenge *of Moving Forward*

"At times I felt like I had to ask my partner's eldest daughter for permission to spend time with him".

"I was excluded from family gatherings ten years after their mother's death because they couldn't handle seeing their father in love with another woman".

"They didn't even live at home. They didn't seem to care how deeply their actions and whispers behind my back hurt me deeply".

When dating a widower, many imagine that the biggest obstacles will come from young, dependent children who might feel threatened or insecure. Yet, surprisingly often, it is the adult children who create the deepest rifts and most complex emotional challenges in a new relationship.

Why does this happen? On the surface, adult children should be mature enough to understand their parents' need for companionship. But real-life family dynamics run deeper than age alone. For adult children, the death of a parent often solidifies the remaining parent as a living link to the family's past. When the widowed parent begins dating, adult children may feel that this threatens the memory of the deceased parent. They might see it as a betrayal not only by their parent but also by anyone new who steps into the family circle.

Unlike minors, who can often adjust with reassurance and consistency, adult children may remain stuck in loyalty conflicts. They might harbour guilt themselves: "If I welcome Dad's new partner, am I disrespecting Mum's memory?" These feelings, if left unspoken, can fester into resentment. Adult children can feel a different kind of possessiveness than minors. As adults, they've shared decades of family stories, holiday traditions, and private jokes that bond them closely to the surviving parent. A new partner can feel like an outsider disrupting this long-established dynamic.

Sometimes, adult children also fear losing influence over their surviving parent. Concerns about inheritance, family traditions, or even everyday decisions can cause them to act defensively. They might try to sabotage the relationship, question your motives, or manipulate their parent with guilt.

In some families, an adult child may unconsciously see themselves as the emotional protector of their widowed parent, as noted in chapter sixteen. When a new partner arrives, this protective instinct can transform into open hostility. They may criticise, exclude, or coldly tolerate your presence. These reactions rarely stem from malice alone. They often come from unresolved grief, fear of change, or fear of their mother being replaced not just in the parent's life, but in the family's story.

Being in a relationship with a widower can be difficult, especially when other people and family members disapprove of the widower's new love interest. Key strategies to help navigate this include:

- Recognise that resistance may come from grief and fear, not pure dislike.
- Encourage open conversations while respecting boundaries.
- Let your partner take the lead in managing family dynamics.
- Avoid competing for loyalty; instead, show genuine care and patience.
- Stay honest about how hostility affects your own emotional health.

Building a future with a widower isn't just about the two of you when children are concerned; it means understanding and gently navigating the existing family tapestry. With adult children, the threads can be more tangled than anyone expects.

Case Study – Laura and Tom

Laura began dating Tom two years after his wife passed away. Tom's youngest daughter, age 10, hesitated at first but eventually warmed to Laura after seeing her father laugh again. However, Tom's adult son, Mark, refused to meet Laura at all, accusing his father of "erasing his mother's memory." Even after two years, he insists that Laura is never to visit the family home while he is there and turned every holiday into an emotional standoff.

Case Study - James and Richard

James fell in love with Richard, a widower whose 25-year-old daughter initially seemed welcoming, but after the engagement began to subtly undermine James. She dismissed him as "just a phase," planned family events without including him, and "forgot" to pass along invitations. Richard felt torn but hesitated to confront his daughter, afraid of damaging their bond. This left James feeling unsure about his place in Richard's life.

Case Study – Sophie and Paul

Steve, Paul's 34-year-old son, took on a caretaker role after his mother died. When Paul began dating Megan, Steve reacted as though Megan's presence threatened not only his late mother's memory but also his place within the family. Steve questioned every decision Megan and Paul made, from travel plans to household purchases, and accused Paul of being "manipulated" when he supported Megan's decisions. The tension nearly ended the relationship until Paul acknowledged his responsibility to set boundaries and engage in family counselling, which allowed Steve to process his grief and begin to accept Megan.

Case Study - Claire and Derek

Derek, widowed after thirty-five years of marriage, began a relationship with Claire, which initially stirred strong emotions in his thirty-two-year-old daughter, Emily. Acting as the self-appointed "guardian of her mother's memory," Emily often steered conversations back to her mother whenever she visited or met her father for lunch or dinner. She compared Claire to her late mother, commenting that "Mum wouldn't have liked that" or "Mum never would have done this," subtly criticising Claire's everyday choices. When

Claire was present, Emily would share old family photos and stories, anchoring interactions firmly in the past. She also resisted Claire's involvement in family traditions, determined to preserve things exactly as they had been.

Eventually, Derek chose to address the tension with honesty and compassion. Through open and heartfelt conversations, he reassured Emily that loving Claire did not diminish her mother. His willingness to validate Emily's grief while also affirming his new relationship created space for healing. Over time, Emily began to see Claire not as a rival but as part of the family's new chapter and a source of her father's happiness.

Recognising the Red Flags

Across these four examples, common patterns emerge that reveal both risks and red flags when dating a widower with adult children. Resistance from adult children often stems not from personal dislike but from grief, loyalty conflicts, and fear of change. Mark's hostility toward Laura demonstrates how unresolved grief can harden into outright rejection, while Richard's daughter's subtle exclusion of James reflects how grief can disguise itself as control. Steve's attempts to micromanage Paul and Megan's relationship show how a child's unprocessed emotions can evolve into manipulation when boundaries are unclear. In contrast, Emily's gradual acceptance of Claire illustrates the power of open communication, reassurance, and emotional leadership.

A key red flag appears when the widower fails to take the lead in managing these complex family dynamics. In Laura's, James's, and Paul's situations, hesitation or guilt left the new partner feeling unsupported, highlighting the need for the widower to actively establish boundaries and balance his children's needs with the integrity of the new relationship. On the other hand, Derek's willingness to address the tension directly, with compassion and honesty, shows how a widower's leadership can shift the family dynamic toward trust, inclusion, and healing.

Family systems experts emphasise that adult children often assume the role of *guardians* of their deceased parent's memory, unconsciously projecting grief, guilt, or loyalty conflicts onto the surviving parent and their new partner [9][25]. This pattern, known as a *loyalty bind*, can cause children to view acceptance of the new partner as an act of betrayal against the deceased parent [17]. Such internal conflict often manifests as resistance, ranging from exclusion and emotional manipulation to overt hostility, which can leave the new partner feeling isolated or undervalued within the family system [4][8].

Grief professionals also note that unresolved grief in both the widower and his children can intensify these conflicts. When the widower avoids setting clear boundaries or fails to assert the new partner's role, adult children may feel required to maintain control of the family narrative, often through subtle or overt acts of rejection [29]. In contrast, when the widower communicates openly, validates his children's grief, and establishes consistent boundaries, the family dynamic tends to stabilise over time, allowing space for mutual respect and adaptation [8].

Research highlights the value of grief counselling for adult children who struggle to accept their parents' new relationship. Therapy provides a safe environment for processing emotions, addressing loyalty conflicts, and understanding that love for a new partner does not diminish love for the deceased [4][17]. It can also support a widower in balancing his parental responsibilities with his commitment to his partner, preventing emotional exhaustion and role confusion for everyone involved.

These case studies and professional insights reveal an underlying truth: the success of a relationship with a widower who has adult children depends heavily on his willingness to lead with clarity and compassion. Clear communication, empathy, and structured boundaries are essential for blending families where grief still lingers. Professionals agree that it is primarily the widower's role to guide this process, while the new partner focuses on maintaining her emotional well-being and self-respect.

It is natural to hope for open arms and acceptance from everyone in the family, but adult children often bring a lifetime of memories, unspoken loyalties, and unresolved grief to the table. Remember, it isn't your job to heal their pain or prove your worthiness. Healthy love requires boundaries, respect, and mutual understanding. The widower must stand beside you, not behind you, and his children must learn that embracing the present does not mean erasing the past. True harmony comes slowly, but with patience, honesty, and courage, new families can find their balance between remembrance and renewal.

Opening the Conversation

When adult children's involvement begins to cause tension, avoidance may feel easier than confronting the issue. Yet silence often reinforces unhealthy dynamics, leaving you feeling unseen or unsupported. Opening the conversation with your partner, honestly, calmly, and with compassion, is an important step in determining whether he is emotionally ready to protect and prioritise your relationship.

Start by focusing on how the situation makes you *feel*, rather than what his children are *doing wrong*. For example:

- "I feel uncomfortable when I'm excluded from family events. It leaves me unsure of where I fit."
- "It's difficult for me when decisions about our home are made without us both being part of the discussion."
- "I want to feel secure in our relationship, but when boundaries aren't clear with your children, I start to doubt my place."

Framing your concerns around your own feelings helps prevent defensiveness and invites empathy. You might also ask reflective questions that encourage mutual understanding and partnership, such as:

- "How do you see our relationship fitting within your family's life?"

- "What role do you think your adult children should have in decisions that affect us both?"
- "How can we make sure everyone feels respected, without sacrificing our connection?"

These questions open space for dialogue rather than debate. However, it's important to recognise that you cannot be the one to manage or mediate his family dynamics. This responsibility rests with the widower. As family therapists note, adult children look to their parent, not a new partner, for cues about what is acceptable [4][8]. When he avoids setting boundaries, it can unintentionally signal that his children's feelings outweigh the stability of the new relationship.

It may help to remind your partner, gently but firmly, that the goal isn't to choose between you and his children, it's to create emotional space for both. For instance:

- "I understand that your children's feelings matter deeply, but I also need to know that our relationship has its own place and respect."

- "I'm not asking you to choose sides. I'm asking you to help create balance, so we both feel valued."

The widower must take the lead in addressing his adult children's over-involvement. When he sets boundaries and communicates expectations clearly, it sends a powerful message: that loving a new partner does not betray the past. It honours growth, healing, and the possibility of a new chapter for everyone.

If he repeatedly refuses to speak up or minimises your concerns, it may indicate that he is not yet ready to balance his past loyalties with his present love. That awareness may hurt, but it can also be empowering; it helps you make decisions based on truth rather than hope.

What to Remember

Silence around grief often deepens conflict, allowing adult children to "gatekeep" the deceased parent's legacy. Open, vulnerable dialogue can help adult children see new partners not as erasers of memory, but as partners in keeping life moving forward. The widower must lead these conversations, balancing loyalty to the past and responsibility to the present.

Chapter 19 - When His Past Enters Your Present

"When I'm not around, he shows my kids photos of his late wife and shares many stories of their life."

"At my daughter's baby shower, he stood up and told the room how his late wife would have loved my daughter dearly".

"Some of my own family members have voiced their concerns about my lack of understanding of his grief and his right to mourn his late wife".

One of the more unexpected situations you might face when dating a widower is his desire for your friends and family to know about his late wife. This request can feel confusing, even hurtful. You may find yourself wondering the same things that I did, "Why should my people learn about someone I never knew? Isn't she part of his past?"

For many widowers, their late wife isn't simply an ex or a chapter that has closed; she remains woven into their identity. He loved, he lost, and he learned or is in the process of learning. These experiences shaped the very qualities you may value in him now: tenderness, empathy, and resilience. Sharing her story isn't always about comparison or reminiscence; sometimes, it's his way of fully revealing himself.

However, it can also reveal something less visible, a sign that he has not yet fully transitioned from mourning to rebuilding and that he is still actively grieving. If his late wife were an ex through divorce and he spoke of her regularly, most people would question whether he was emotionally ready to love again. The same theory applies to widowers: grief may differ from divorce, but emotional availability matters just as much. A widower who still needs others to validate his bond with his past may not yet be ready to invest fully in the present.

A widower who seeks reassurance from his new partner's friends and family can unintentionally create tension, leaving the partner feeling overlooked or uncertain about her place in the relationship. Honouring a widower's late wife can be a natural and caring part of his life, but challenges may arise if the new partner is consistently expected to prioritise or celebrate the deceased at every gathering, holiday, or milestone.

After I separated from Bill, I found out that Bill either mentioned or showed pictures of his late wife to my family at every family get-together when I wasn't in the room. In some cases, like mine, widowers may still strongly identify with their role as a partner to their late wife, making it harder to fully embrace their present relationship. When grief shapes interactions, and your family and friends are expected to honour someone they haven't met, family gatherings can feel weighed down by the past rather than being opportunities for shared connection, placing an emotional burden on everyone involved.

As Pauline Boss reminds us, ambiguous loss does not resolve itself neatly with time; it lingers in the uneasy space between holding on and letting go. In this light, a widower's wish for your friends and family to know about his late wife can be understood as an attempt to live in both worlds at once. He may be seeking quiet reassurance that his ongoing bond is permissible, that he can honour what was without being forced to erase it.

Yet when that bond begins to dominate the story, when his late wife becomes a recurring presence in conversations, introductions, or family dynamics, it can point to something more unresolved. Rather than having integrated his grief, he may still be anchored to it, emotionally unavailable to make genuine room for a new relationship to take shape.

In family systems theory, grief is not experienced in isolation; it circulates through the family network, influencing relationships, roles, and boundaries [33]. Integrating past and present within these systems helps reduce emotional conflict and allows new connections to form without resentment or confusion. For a widower, sharing his history with your family and friends may feel like a way to bridge past and present: he hopes they will understand how his experiences shaped him, and that loving you is not a betrayal of his late wife.

Even when you intellectually grasp these intentions, the request for your loved ones to "know" his late wife can stir complex emotions. You may feel secondary, fearing comparisons or idealisation that leave you feeling like a placeholder. Boundaries can blur, making your safe spaces feel partially claimed by someone else. You might sense invisible pressure, silently tasked with upholding a memory that isn't yours to preserve, a responsibility you never agreed to carry. These feelings are valid and reflect your own need for emotional safety and belonging.

Case study - Alicia and Tom

Alicia and Tom had been together for just over a year when Tom asked whether her sister, who lived nearby, might like to see some photos of his late wife, Sandra. The request caught Alicia off guard. She wasn't sure why Tom wanted to share images of his past with her family, and she worried her sister might draw comparisons or feel unsure about how to respond.

When they discussed it, Alicia learned that Tom's intention wasn't to centre Sandra, but to help Alicia's family understand the loss that continued to shape parts of his life. He hoped that by offering this context, they might better understand why he sometimes hesitated with plans or found certain dates emotionally complicated. Even with this explanation, Alicia felt conflicted. She cared for Tom deeply, but moments like this made her wonder whether he was fully anchored in their present relationship.

At a small family dinner, Tom shared a few memories and brought out a small packet of photos he had tucked into his jacket. Alicia's sister listened kindly and asked thoughtful questions, and soon the conversation shifted into Tom's past. For Tom, the moment felt like an act of honesty and trust. For Alicia, it reinforced a quiet ache, a sense of being overshadowed yet again, especially since she had never felt the need, or been invited, to share stories or photos of her former partner with Tom's family.

Case Study - David and Grace

Grace, 61, had been with David, 64, a widower, for two years. David lost his wife, Margaret, a decade earlier. Early in their relationship, Grace welcomed his stories, and they kept a photo of Margaret in a shared living space.

As the relationship grew, Grace gently suggested it might help to reserve special commemorations for Margaret's birthday or the anniversary of her passing rather than including a toast to her at every holiday dinner with her adult children.

David felt hurt but said little. Secretly, however, he spoke to Grace's two grown daughters, telling them he was "worried" about Grace's "coldness" and asking if they felt she was being unfair. He framed his sadness as evidence that Grace didn't truly love him "as he is."

Grace's daughters felt uncomfortable but also conflicted. They quietly began questioning Grace's motives, wondering if she was being insensitive. Grace later discovered the conversation had happened behind her back. She felt betrayed not only by David's words but by the fact that he brought her children into a conflict that should have stayed between the two of them.

The family dynamic shifted: dinners felt tense, and Grace sensed she had to "prove" she cared. Instead of feeling closer, the couple drifted apart, as trust eroded.

Recognising the Red Flags

Dating a widower can bring unexpected challenges, particularly when his grief and past relationships enter the present. Alicia and Grace's experiences illustrate how a widower's desire to share memories of a late spouse can impact a new relationship. While these gestures often stem from vulnerability and a need to be understood, the consequences for the new partner can vary significantly. For Alicia, Tom's wish to show her family photos of his late wife left her feeling overshadowed and displaced. For Grace, David's decision to speak to her adult children about perceived coldness created a sense of betrayal and eroded trust.

Across these stories, clear red flags emerge:

- When a widower's grief is projected into social circles, leaving the new partner feeling secondary or emotionally sidelined.

- When private grief is shared with friends or family rather than discussed directly with the partner, it can create unintended loyalty conflicts or emotional triangles.

- When the widower seeks validation for his grief from the new partner's social network, he is subtly shifting responsibility for his emotional state.

- When remembrance crosses into control, manipulation, or performance, such as expecting the new partner to uphold rituals, celebrate the deceased at gatherings, or manage others' perceptions of the past.

In Alicia and Tom's case, Tom intended to foster empathy, helping Alicia's family understand the depth of his loss. While this reflected transparency and trust, it also highlighted how public displays of grief can make a new partner feel emotionally displaced. Grace and David's story shows the more damaging effects when grief becomes a tool for control: by involving Grace's adult daughters, David blurred boundaries, created tension, and turned private emotions into a test of loyalty.

Professional insight helps explain what's going on. These experts note that widowers may remain anchored in the identity of being a partner to their late wife, especially when they have not fully accepted their loss [4][33]. Sharing memories or involving others in these stories is not always harmful, but when it dominates connections or damages the new partner's sense of belonging, it can signal unresolved grief and an imbalance in emotional prioritisation [5].

Research also highlights the psychological impact on new partners. Being placed in a position of managing the widower's grief, defending boundaries, or competing with memory can cause stress, insecurity, and a sense of invisibility [4][9]. When a widower does not take responsibility for balancing past and present, he is intentionally or unintentionally creating an environment where his new partner's needs and emotions are not being considered.

A healthy approach requires integration rather than dominance. Widowers should acknowledge their past but share it in ways that do not overshadow the present relationship. Open communication between partners, clear boundaries around when and how grief is expressed, or professional support for both parties can prevent the past from becoming a source of control or exclusion. As James Worden notes, "Love after loss doesn't mean choosing one over the other; it means finding space for the past while living fully in the present" [4].

For new partners, the takeaway is clear: the red flags are not about grief itself, but how it is managed. Signs that caution is needed include: feeling secondary in social or family settings, being asked to uphold a stranger's memory, witnessing private grief shared publicly in ways that compromise boundaries, or noticing that the widower is not actively supporting your emotional presence in the relationship. When these patterns appear, they may be signs that the widower may not yet be emotionally available.

Ultimately, a balanced relationship honours both history and the current partnership. The past can be acknowledged and remembered, but it should never overshadow the present or place the new partner in a position of emotional labour she did not choose.

A healthy approach recognises that true intimacy grows when both partners acknowledge histories, protect the present, and build a future together, holding the past in one hand while offering the other to the living relationship.

Recognising the red flags matters. When a widower's grief dominates social interactions, when he seeks constant validation, or imposes loyalty tests, it can often signal that he is emotionally attached to his previous relationship rather than fully present in the one he is trying to build with you. Naming these patterns early gives women the language to protect their emotional safety, to set and hold firm boundaries, and to choose relationships grounded in mutual respect, empathy, and emotional availability.

Opening the Conversation

Discussing how a widower's grief affects your relationship can feel delicate, but approaching it thoughtfully can prevent misunderstandings and strengthen your connection. The goal is to share your experience without making him feel blamed or attacked.

Focus on the impact, not the intent. Rather than telling him what he is doing wrong, explain how certain situations affect you emotionally. For example:

- "When stories of your late wife come up during family gatherings, I sometimes feel unsure of my place and unsure how to respond."

- "I notice that I struggle to participate fully when past memories dominate our time together."

Framing concerns in terms of emotional impact helps him understand your perspective and opens the door for collaboration.

Collaborate on solutions. Invite him to explore ways to balance remembrance with the present. Questions like:

- "How can we share your past in a way that feels comfortable for both of us?"
- "What boundaries could help ensure that your grief and our relationship coexist peacefully?" These prompts encourage joint problem-solving rather than conflict.

Highlight his role in setting boundaries. It's important to gently remind him that managing grief and family dynamics is his responsibility. For instance:

- "It would help if you could guide conversations with your children or family so that I don't feel caught in the middle."

- "Your leadership can make it easier for all of us to honour the past while prioritising the present."

When friends or family are involved in preserving memories, coordinate with your partner before engaging with them. Strategies include:

- Agree on how and when stories, photos, or commemorations will be shared.
- Discuss in advance any gatherings where the past may be brought into focus.
- Keep communication lines clear, so you feel supported rather than overshadowed.

Couples or family counselling can provide a structured space to discuss grief, boundaries, and expectations [4][33]. Professional support helps ensure that both partners' emotional needs are respected and that past and present can coexist without conflict.

What to Remember

Healthy remembrance honours the past, whereas a healthy partnership protects the present. The goal is neither forgetting nor forever performing grief but building a shared life where the living, too, feel free to celebrate, laugh, and fully belong.

Chapter 20 - The Late Wife's Family

"I never felt accepted by his late wife's family and didn't appreciate being compared and criticised by them either."

"I felt like an outsider, as though my feelings didn't exist, and that their world would be better if I wasn't in it."

"Being told I would never be as good as his late wife stung like a million bees."

It can come as a shock when a widower's late wife's parents, siblings, or extended relatives become openly critical or quietly obstructive of his new relationship. Sometimes the interference is overt: hurtful remarks, exclusion of the new partner at family events, or guilt-laden reminders of "what she would have wanted." Other times, it's subtle: coldness, silence, or emotional distance that makes the new partner feel forever outside the circle of belonging.

This behaviour is rarely driven by simple jealousy or cruelty. More often, it arises from a complex web of love, loyalty, grief, and fear. After a death, families reorganise themselves around the memory of the deceased. The late wife's parents or siblings may still see the widower as "hers," part of their ongoing family identity. His decision to love again can feel like a threat, not only to her memory, but to their shared sense of who they are as a family.

From conversations with women who have dated widowers, it's clear that the late wife's relatives often cling to him as a living link to their loved one. The new partner then becomes the outsider, a visible reminder that life is moving forward without the person they still mourn. Some family members see themselves as guardians of the late wife's memory, protecting her legacy by monitoring or judging how quickly the widower moves on. In their eyes, they're honouring her, but to the new partner, it feels like being compared to someone she can never equal.

When children are involved, the situation often becomes more complicated. The late wife's family may fear that a new partner and their family will "replace" them as grandparents, aunts, or uncles. They can worry that the children will grow closer to the new partner's family, leaving them behind. That fear can drive subtle or overt interference: making passive-aggressive remarks, undermining the new partner's authority, or urging the widower to "keep the relationship quiet for now." For the new partner, the effects can be deeply painful. She may feel:

- Compared to someone she can never compete with.
- Excluded from important family occasions or decisions.
- Pressured to prove her loyalty to a woman she never met.

- Resentful that the widower doesn't draw clearer boundaries.

Over time, these dynamics can erode trust. A widower's new partner may question whether he can truly stand beside her, while he may feel torn between loyalty to the past and responsibility to the present.

Case Study – Daniel and Marianne

Daniel, 62, began dating Marianne, 58, three years after losing his wife, Ellen. In the early days, Ellen's sister, Carol, seemed genuinely supportive. She checked in often, welcomed Marianne politely, and appeared to accept that Daniel was finding happiness again. But as the relationship deepened and the couple became engaged, Carol's behaviour shifted.

Subtle comments began to creep in. She started referring to Marianne as "the new one". One day, Carol looked Marianne up and down and remarked that Ellen never wore makeup or heels as she was naturally beautiful. Each comment felt like a comparison, leaving Marianne constantly aware of the woman who came before her.

One evening, Carol phoned Daniel and said, "I know you still love Ellen; you don't have to prove anything to her." The call was on the loudspeaker, and Marianne overheard. Her words carried an emotional weight, a reminder that, in Carol's eyes, Ellen still held centre stage.

Over time, Daniel came to understand what was happening. During Ellen's illness, Carol had been his emotional anchor, the person he turned to when fear, exhaustion, and grief felt too heavy to carry alone. She had stepped into that role out of love for her sister, and in many ways, had remained there long after Ellen passed. As Daniel began building a future with Marianne, Carol still clung to the past, unable to step out of the position she once occupied.

Case Study – Annie and Geoff

Annie and Geoff had been dating for two years when Geoff proposed. Excited for their future, they eagerly shared the news with family and friends. Geoff's adult children were delighted, and both families offered their blessings. Wanting to include everyone, Geoff shared the news with his late wife's sister, Robyn, a professional wedding planner. Robyn offered to plan their wedding for free.

Annie was hesitant at first, but later agreed, thinking it would be a kind gesture to include the children's beloved aunt. However, just weeks before the wedding, Robyn unveiled her "plans": she had arranged for an empty chair at the bridal table to honour her sister, changed the flowers to her sister's favourite, sunflowers, and added a full-page photo of her to the wedding program. Annie felt blindsided and hurt, as though her own role in the celebration had been diminished.

When Annie tried to express her discomfort, Robyn took offence and withdrew from the planning altogether, sending Geoff a bill for her time. The wedding eventually went ahead with the help of Annie's friends, who stepped in to help. The incident left a lasting scar, a reminder of how his late wife's family's grief overshadowed his new beginnings.

Case Study – Maureen

Maureen had been in a loving relationship with Alan, a father to a 17-year-old son, for over two years. Alan's late wife passed away six years before they met. They were planning to sell their homes and buy one together, a step that symbolised the new life they were both hoping to build. Alan remained close to his late wife's family, and from early on, Maureen noticed that they persistently left her out of family events. She was excluded from Christmas, birthday and family gatherings, including Alan and his son's birthday celebrations; they also held memorials for Alan's late wife on both her birthday and the anniversary of her passing.

When Alan shared his intention to propose, the reaction from his late wife's family was immediate and harsh. They accused him of "erasing" their daughter's memory, insisted he was moving on too quickly, and made it clear they did not want Maureen involved in their lives. They even suggested that their daughter would not have approved of Maureen helping to raise Alan's son, a comment that cut deeply, even though it was grounded in their own grief and fear of change.

The pressure soon became unbearable. Caught between loyalty to his late wife's family and his love for Maureen, Alan grew increasingly withdrawn and began spending more and more time with his former in-laws. Maureen found herself questioning whether love alone could withstand the emotional pull they still held over him.

The turning point came on the anniversary of his late wife's death, when Alan attended a memorial event organised by her family, an event Maureen learned about after the fact. It crystallised the painful truth: Alan was still deeply entangled in his past, and the boundaries needed to protect their relationship simply weren't being set.

Under the weight of conflicting loyalties and unspoken expectations, their relationship eventually collapsed.

Case Study – Paula

Paula married Stan, a widower with three children, and later adopted the children, hoping to create a united, harmonious family. Yet Stan's late wife's relatives struggled to accept her. Their disapproval was obvious: they attended family events but barely acknowledged Paula, made negative comments about her to the children, and even spread rumours of infidelity when she became pregnant.

Stan hesitated to set boundaries, worried about jeopardising his children's connection with their maternal relatives. As a result, Paula felt increasingly unsupported and invisible within the family. Only when Stan recognised the toll the situation was taking on their marriage did he take action, stepping in to establish boundaries and limit contact, creating space for their new family to thrive.

Recognising the Red Flags

Across these stories and the psychological insights woven through them, one theme becomes unmistakably clear: grief rarely stays contained within the widower. It often ripples through the entire family system, shaping dynamics, loyalties, and unspoken expectations in ways that deeply affect the new partner. Whether it appears as interference, exclusion, blurred boundaries, or confusion about roles, the emotional residue of the past relationship can quietly, and sometimes loudly, intrude on the present.

In Daniel's and Annie's stories, the late wife's relatives continued to treat her memory as the emotional centre of the family system. Everything still seemed to orbit around the deceased, and the widower's new partner was subtly positioned in her shadow. This ongoing centring of the past signalled that the family had not yet shifted into a new chapter. In Maureen's and Paula's experiences, the interference was quieter but just as painful: being left out of gatherings, feeling unwelcome at family celebrations, or sensing an unspoken refusal to acknowledge them as part of the widower's life. These forms of exclusion made it clear that the family had not emotionally opened its doors to the future.

Another recurring pattern was the way some family members held tightly to roles that should naturally evolve. Relatives who had once been emotional confidantes, advisers, or gatekeepers during the late wife's life sometimes continue acting in these positions long after the widower has started a new relationship. Whether through unsolicited advice, decision-making overreach, or emotional dependence, these blurred boundaries made it difficult for the new partner to form her own place in the widower's world. The family's grip on old roles often reflected unresolved grief, but it still created instability for the emerging partnership.

One of the most emotionally corrosive dynamics was the repetition of comparisons to the late wife. Comments about how she would have behaved, or what she would have preferred, placed the new partner in an impossible position. These comparisons reinforced an idealised memory that no living person could ever match. Alongside these comparisons were more subtle forms of emotional pressure, guilt-based statements such as "She wouldn't have liked this" or "Don't forget what she meant to us." These remarks were often presented as expressions of loyalty, but they kept the widower anchored in the past and left his partner feeling evaluated through someone else's lens.

A deeper psychological explanation helps illuminate why these patterns emerge. Grief expert J. William Worden describes one essential task of mourning as the ability to emotionally relocate the deceased and move on with life [4]. This doesn't mean forgetting the person who died; it means holding their memory in a way that doesn't intrude on new relationships. When this emotional relocation has not occurred, whether for the widower or his late wife's family, the past remains alive in ways that shape the present. This often shows up as rituals, memorial expectations, family decisions, and everyday interactions that reflect the emotional weight of a life that once was rather than the life unfolding now.

Family systems theory further explains why unresolved grief can affect the new partner so intensely. Dr Murray Bowen's concept of triangulation describes situations where the widower becomes caught between the needs of his new partner and the expectations of the late wife's family. This emotional tug-of-war rarely resolves itself; instead, it preserves imbalance. The widower may feel torn between two emotional worlds, particularly if he fears disappointing his late wife's relatives or being perceived as disloyal. His struggle to balance these loyalties is itself a red flag, signalling that boundaries are unclear and that grief is still shaping key decisions in his current relationship.

For the new partner, these dynamics often create a painful sense of emotional invisibility. She may begin to feel unseen, unheard, or overshadowed, not because of who she is, but because the space she is trying to enter is still occupied by the past. When family rituals, memorial traditions, or daily conversations revolve more around what once was than what is, it becomes clear that the past is dictating the emotional rhythm of the present.

Perhaps the most significant indicator of all is the widower's difficulty in setting healthy boundaries. When he avoids addressing exclusion, remains silent in the face of comparisons, or leaves his partner to navigate uncomfortable family dynamics alone, it highlights his struggle to differentiate, to honour the past while protecting and prioritising the present. Without active boundary-setting, the relationship remains vulnerable to emotional overreach from the outside forces and to loyalty conflicts within the widower himself.

It's important to recognise that most of these behaviours are not born from malice. Families who were deeply bonded to the late wife may fear being forgotten or losing their significance. Their grief is real. Empathy for their pain can coexist alongside the recognition that their behaviours, even the subtle ones, can be deeply damaging. Understanding their grief does not require the new partner to tolerate ongoing hurt, exclusion, or imbalance.

Opening the Conversation

Talking about how a widower's grief and family involvement impacts your relationship can feel sensitive, but approaching the conversation thoughtfully can prevent misunderstandings and help you both feel more connected. The aim is to share your experience without placing blame.

Focus on the impact, not the intent. Explain how certain situations affect you emotionally. For example:

- "I feel uncomfortable when family gatherings revolve around comparisons to your late wife."
- "I notice I feel excluded when I'm left out of events or decisions that involve your family."

- "I sometimes feel overshadowed when stories of your late wife dominate conversations at family gatherings."

Framing concerns in terms of emotional impact helps him understand your perspective and encourages collaboration. Collaborate on solutions. Invite him to explore ways to balance remembrance with the present. Questions like:

- "How can we include your late wife's family's memories in a way that still honours our relationship?"
- "What boundaries would make it easier for both of us to feel comfortable at family events?"
- "How can we navigate comments or comparisons to the past without them affecting us?"
- These prompts invite joint problem-solving rather than blame.

Highlight his role in setting boundaries. Gently remind him that managing grief and family dynamics is primarily his responsibility. For instance:

- "It would help if you could guide conversations with your children or relatives, so I don't feel caught in the middle."
- "Your leadership can ensure that your past is honoured while our present relationship remains strong."
- "Let's decide together how to handle family expectations or comments that may feel hurtful."

Coordinate with family and friends before engaging with them directly. Strategies include agreeing on how and when stories, photos, or commemorations will be shared, and discussing in advance gatherings where the past may be highlighted. Keep communication lines clear, so you feel supported rather than sidelined.

What to Remember

Healthy love after loss isn't about choosing one family over another. It's about creating a life where the past is respected but not allowed to rule the present. When grief remains unhealed, the late wife's family can unknowingly hold everyone hostage to the past. For healing to occur, the widower must find the courage to step out of triangulation and establish emotional boundaries that allow new love to flourish, without guilt, secrecy, or apology.

Chapter 21 - Social Ties That Keep Grief Alive

"I ended up making excuses because I didn't want to go somewhere where I didn't feel welcome".

"I sometimes felt like I was wearing the wrong team colours and that I was doing the wrong thing by trying to enjoy myself"

"I had my own set of friends and was happy to make new ones, but I didn't like the feeling of having to jump through hoops to prove myself as worthy enough to be befriended".

Dating or marrying a widower often brings unexpected challenges beyond the home. Social circles, clubs, or community networks that were established during his marriage can create subtle, but powerful, barriers to a new partner's sense of belonging. These groups may still hold strong emotional ties to the past, struggling to welcome someone new, and the new partner can feel judged, excluded, or invisible despite the widower's best intentions.

In this chapter, we explore why these dynamics occur, the psychological effects on the new partner, and how a widower can honour past loyalties while creating a secure space for his present relationship. We will examine real-life case studies and expert insights to illustrate these challenges and provide practical strategies for navigating social circles shaped by loss.

Case Study - Claire and the Social Club

Claire had been dating Mark, a widower, for nearly a year when he invited her to join the sailing club he had shared with his late wife for over two decades. Claire felt nervous but hopeful about being welcomed into his social circle. Instead, she found herself subtly frozen out: club members would reminisce fondly about Mark's late wife, sharing inside jokes and stories where Claire could not contribute.

One member, who had been the late wife's closest friend, openly questioned why Mark had moved on "so soon" and asked Claire what her intentions with Mark really were. At events, Claire's presence was treated almost like an intrusion, and she overheard someone whisper that welcoming her would dishonour the memory of Mark's late wife. Over time, Claire began to dread attending club gatherings, feeling judged and invisible despite Mark's reassurances.

Case Study - Emily and the School Association

Emily married Daniel, a widower with two young children, six months ago. Daniels' late wife had passed away four years prior, and Emily had been actively parenting the children for two years and was in the process of formally adopting them. Despite her commitment, Emily felt deeply excluded by the parent-teacher association at the children's school, where Daniels' late wife had once played an influential role.

Whenever Emily offered suggestions or participated in meetings, some long-standing members would curtly remind her, "That's not what Sarah would have wanted." Others whispered about how quickly Daniel had remarried. Emily felt heartbroken and undermined, particularly as her ideas were meant to benefit the children she now loved and cared for daily. The subtle and overt reminders of the late wife's preferences made Emily feel like an outsider, constantly battling the ghost of someone she never met but who continued to dominate community decisions and expectations.

Recognising the Red Flags

Claire and Emily's stories reveal the complex social dimensions of dating or marrying a widower, in which grief extends beyond the home into the broader community. These examples illustrate what happens when the late wife's social world, friends, clubs, and community networks, resist making space for the new partner. While the contexts differ, the emotional impact is strikingly similar: the new partner becomes a guest in a life still arranged around the deceased's memory.

In Claire's story, exclusion unfolds in a public, almost ritualised setting: the sailing club once shared by Mark and his late wife. The club members, particularly the late wife's close friends, act as gatekeepers of grief, policing who is allowed to belong and what constitutes loyalty. Claire's attempts to integrate are subtly undermined through comparison, gossip, and reminders of the past. Despite Mark's best intentions, he underestimates how powerfully group loyalty can sustain emotional allegiance to the deceased, leaving Claire feeling invisible. Her experience highlights the social inheritance of grief, where shared mourning becomes an ongoing act of identity for those left behind, sometimes at the expense of the living.

Emily's experience, though in a different environment, reflects similar dynamics. The parent-teacher association's attachment to Daniel's late wife's legacy creates an invisible hierarchy that Emily can never fully enter. Each time someone reminds her of "what Sarah would have wanted," Daniel's late wife's memory becomes a moral benchmark against which Emily is measured. This form of "comparative grief loyalty" keeps her in a perpetual state of emotional competition, not because of anything she has done wrong, but because the community has not yet processed its own loss. Even her caregiving and love for the children are insufficient to earn belonging, as the group continues to define family and identity through the lens of the deceased.

These cases demonstrate recurring red flags for new partners navigating widower social circles:

1. The deceased remains the emotional centre of social spaces. New partners can be measured against the late wife's memory, leaving them feeling undervalued or invisible [4].

2. Blurring of boundaries and roles. Friends or relatives continue acting as advisers, gatekeepers, or emotional confidantes long after the marriage ends, undermining the new partner's role.

3. Exclusion from gatherings or decision-making. Being left out of community events can signal that the new partner is not fully accepted.

4. Comparisons to the late wife. Comments about how the deceased would have acted or what she preferred place the new partner in an impossible, evaluative position [26].

5. Guilt-based pressure or loyalty enforcement. Statements such as "That's not what she would have wanted" subtly maintain emotional anchoring to the past.

6. Widower caught between competing loyalties. Triangulation occurs when the widower struggles to satisfy both the new partner and the social network linked to his late wife.

7. Emotional invisibility or overshadowing. New partners may feel unseen, unheard, or unimportant when community and family interactions are dominated by memories of the deceased.

From a psychological perspective, unresolved grief in social networks can leave both the widower and his new partner emotionally stuck. Grief expert J. William Worden describes the essential task of mourning as the ability to emotionally relocate the deceased and move on with life [4].

Family systems theory further explains that when unresolved grief persists, triangulation can occur, leaving the widower torn between his new partner and loyalty to the deceased's social circle [26].

Ultimately, these dynamics point to a deeper truth: love after loss is not sustained by emotional healing alone. It also requires a conscious reshaping of the social world that surrounds the widower. For a new relationship to breathe and grow, both he and those around him must be willing to make room for the living, understanding that honouring what was should never come at the cost of sidelining what is.

Opening the Conversation

Raising the topic of social circles' overinvolvement and unprocessed grief can feel awkward, but it's essential for building a secure partnership. The goal is to express your experience without blaming your partner.

Focus on the impact, not the intent:

- "When your late wife's club member friends make comparisons during gatherings, I sometimes feel unsure of my place."
- "I notice that I struggle to feel fully included when past memories dominate community events."

Collaborate on solutions:

- "How can we share the past in a way that feels comfortable for both of us?"
- "What boundaries could help ensure that other people's grief and our relationship coexist peacefully?"

Highlight his role in setting boundaries:

- "It would help if you could guide these conversations so that I don't feel caught in the middle."
- "Your leadership in this can make it easier to honour the past while prioritising the present."

What to Remember

Loyalty to a widower's late wife can unintentionally harm his new partner's self-esteem and confidence by denying them recognition and respect. The widower must realise that his club and social settings may feel familiar to him, but may feel exclusive to the person he now loves.

Chapter 22 - Pressure to Be a Different Version of You

"They expected me to continue her traditions, but I had my own. I felt like there was no room for me unless I stepped into her shadow."

"They kept telling me, 'She always did it this way,' and all I could think was, But I'm not her."

"His daughter told me I should learn her mother's recipes so things could 'feel normal again.' That broke something in me."

In this chapter, we explore the complex and often painful dynamics that emerge when a widower's new partner feels pressured by family, friends, or even the widower himself to step into the role once held by the late wife. This pressure can be subtle or overt and manifest in a variety of ways, such as being asked to cook the same meals, host gatherings the same way, or embrace the late wife's hobbies, traditions, and social roles. Often, these expectations are not born of malice but stem from unresolved grief, nostalgia, or a desire to recreate a lost sense of family or social harmony.

The emotional impact on the new partner can be profound. She may feel that she is never fully loved for who she is but valued only for how closely she resembles someone from the past. Through real-life stories, psychological insights, and expert commentary, this chapter examines why these dynamics occur and how they can unintentionally stall both the widower's healing and the development of a healthy relationship that is focused on the present.

For the new partner, these pressures, often unintentional, can still be deeply damaging, potentially leading to feelings of resentment, loss of self-identity, and emotional burnout. This chapter also offers practical strategies for establishing boundaries, asserting identity within the relationship, and opening honest conversations about each partner's needs and desires, separate from the shadows of the past.

Case Study: Olivia and James

Olivia started dating a widower named James. Early in their relationship, James's adult daughters encouraged Olivia to cook their mother's favourite dishes and keep the house the way their mother did. James suggested that Olivia could wear jewellery that belonged to his late wife and wear clothing that his late wife would wear.

James often reminisced about how his late wife hosted holidays, subtly suggesting Olivia could do the same. Over time, though she wanted to support him, Olivia felt her individuality slipping away and questioned whether James truly loved her or merely missed what he had lost.

Olivia realised that she was living in the shadow of James' previous life, rather than building a new life together. Olivia tried to communicate her concerns with James, who suggested that Olivia was being insensitive to his grief and that she was merely jealous of the relationship that he had with his late wife.

James's assumptions, coupled with Olivia feeling that her concerns were not being heard and misunderstood, led Oliva to realise that James was not able to meet her emotional needs and decided to end the relationship.

Case Study: Sally and John

Sally had been seeing John for six months, and although they weren't living together, she was hopeful about where the relationship was heading. That hope dimmed when John began encouraging her to keep his late wife's designer label clothes and wear her perfume. He framed it as a way to honour his late wife's memory, feel closer to his family, and ensure that the items were "used rather than thrown away."

At first, Sally tried to be understanding. She wanted to support him in his grief. But felt overwhelmed at the thought of wearing another woman's clothes and perfume. Sally thought that the scent and the clothes symbolised as a constant reminder of a life she had not lived, each one made her feel as though she was being compared to someone she could never be. She wore the perfume once, but instead of feeling welcomed into John's world, she felt like an imposter in her own.

As time went on, Sally began to feel invisible, as if her own identity didn't matter and her presence was valued only for how closely she could mirror the late wife. The pressure created confusion and sadness, and she found herself questioning whether John truly wanted *her* or simply a living echo of the past.

Eventually, Sally realised she was being asked to live in a way that felt deeply uncomfortable, and she began to see other signs that John was not ready for a new relationship.

With clarity and courage, she chose to walk away, protecting her sense of self and acknowledging that love cannot grow where individuality is replaced by someone else's memory.

Case Study- Donna and Chad

Donna had been in a loving, balanced relationship with Chad for eight months. Chad was the president of the local football club and rarely missed a weekend match. Although Donna knew very little about football, she enjoyed spending time with him and happily went along to support the team.

One Sunday, a woman from the club approached her. She introduced herself as Maureen and, without much preamble, asked Donna if she would be willing to work in the canteen. Maureen explained that Chad's late wife had been the canteen manager for years and had helped out every Sunday. Since her passing, they had struggled to fill the role. She added that Chad would 'love' Donna to be more involved in the club's activities.

Donna froze. She knew instantly that she didn't want to work in the canteen, let alone manage it. Cooking wasn't something she enjoyed, and the idea of stepping into the exact role once filled by Chad's late wife felt deeply uncomfortable. She thanked Maureen politely and said she would think about it.

After the game, Donna told Chad what had happened. Chad laughed and admitted that Maureen often lacked a filter. He acknowledged how awkward the situation must have felt for Donna. Donna made it clear that she would not be running any canteens; she joked that she "could probably burn water." Chad reassured her that he understood.

At the next game, Chad stayed close to Donna, knowing Maureen would likely return for an answer. As expected, Maureen approached them again. But before she could say a word, Chad politely stepped in. He asked Maureen if *she* could take on managing the canteen and offered to help her find volunteers to support her. Maureen immediately agreed, thanked Chad, and headed back toward the canteen. Donna felt relieved.

Case Study - Robin and Simon

Robin had been in a strong, loving relationship with Simon for almost two years when an unexpected conversation left her feeling blindsided. One afternoon, Simon's sister, Sue, approached Robin and casually asked whether she would be hosting Christmas that year.

Robin was taken aback. She and Simon had only been living together for two months, and last Christmas they had split the day between Simon's eldest daughter's home for lunch and Robin's son's home for dinner. Hosting had never even been discussed.

Sue didn't hesitate to elaborate. She explained that Christmas "just hadn't been the same" since Simon's late wife passed away, and that the holiday belonged at Simon's house. She went on to detail the elaborate effort Simon's late wife put in each year: the family's favourite dishes she cooked, the beautifully decorated home, the traditions she upheld. Sue then added, almost as an instruction, that Robin would "need to make the family favourites this year so no one is disappointed."

Robin felt a knot form in her stomach. The expectation wasn't just to host, it was to duplicate another woman's Christmas, right down to her recipes, decorations, and traditions. She barely knew where anything was kept in the house and did not want to step into a role loaded with nostalgia and grief.

Later that evening, Robin shared the conversation with Simon. To her relief, Simon was empathetic and immediately recognised how unfair the request had been. He told Robin he had no intention of hosting Christmas that year and that the pressure being placed on her was unreasonable.

When Simon relayed this to Sue, the situation escalated. Sue became defensive and accused Robin of influencing his decision. She insisted that if Simon's late wife were alive, she would "never be so miserable" and would gladly host Christmas for the entire family. Sue framed Robin as the problem, suggesting that she was disrupting long-standing family traditions rather than acknowledging that those traditions were built around a woman Robin could never, and should never, be expected to replace.

The exchange left Robin feeling both relieved to have Simon's support and saddened by Sue's reaction. It highlighted how easily some people project their grief onto the new partner, expecting her to carry traditions that belonged to someone else. It also showed the importance of a widower recognising these pressures and setting boundaries to protect the well-being of their new relationship.

Recognising the Red Flags

The stories of Olivia, Sally, Donna, and Robin reveal a deeply important truth about relationships with widowers: pressure on the new partner rarely comes from one direction. Instead, it emerges from a mix of unresolved grief, family expectations, social habits, and sometimes the widower's own difficulty separating the past from the present. While each woman's experience unfolded in a different context, the underlying patterns are strikingly similar, and they offer clear indicators of when a relationship may be drifting into emotionally unsafe territory.

One of the clearest red flags is the expectation for the new partner to replicate the late wife. This can appear subtly, as it did for Olivia, who was encouraged to cook the late wife's favourite meals and even wear her jewellery. Or it can be overt, like in Sally's case, where she was urged to wear the late wife's perfume and designer clothing. These gestures are often framed as "honouring her memory," but underneath lies an implicit comparison that erodes the new partner's individuality. Psychology research shows that this behaviour often stems from unresolved grief, where people unconsciously cling to familiarity to soothe emotional discomfort rather than embracing the uniqueness of a new relationship.

A second red flag is what many women describe as identity erosion, the slow fading of their sense of self under the weight of someone else's history. Olivia began to feel as though she was living in a life already scripted by another woman, never truly loved for who she was. Sally described feeling like an imposter in her own relationship, wearing symbols that didn't belong to her and being asked to embody a memory rather than show up as herself. When the late wife becomes the yardstick against which the new partner is measured, emotional safety starts to dissolve.

In other situations, red flags arise through social or community pressure to take over the late wife's roles. Donna experienced this within the football club, where a well-intentioned but insensitive club member asked her to manage the canteen "just like Chad's late wife did." The assumption was simple but harmful: that Donna should naturally step into a role that was never hers to begin with. Robin faced a similar pressure from Simon's sister, Sue, who attempted to assign her the late wife's Christmas duties, from hosting the entire family to cooking the traditional dishes and decorating the home in the exact same way. These situations reveal a broader pattern: communities often struggle to emotionally "update" their roles after a loss, leaving the new partner caught in a system still structured around the deceased.

Another significant red flag is the dismissal of the new partner's discomfort. When Olivia expressed her concerns to James, she was told she was being insensitive and even accused of jealousy. The message was clear: the late wife's needs mattered more than Olivia's emotional reality. This kind of minimisation creates an unsafe relational environment where the new partner feels unable to express boundaries without backlash or judgement. In Robin's situation, while Simon responded compassionately, his sister weaponised grief by blaming Robin for disrupting family traditions, reinforcing the emotional hierarchy that placed the deceased at the centre of all decisions.

Family involvement can also create loyalty traps, where the new partner is expected to uphold traditions or roles connected to the late wife. While these expectations often arise from genuine grief or a desire to preserve family identity, they can leave the new partner feeling like a placeholder rather than a valued member of the family. When family members, like Sue or Maureen, use nostalgia or obligation to pressure the new partner, it becomes a sign that the emotional ecosystem surrounding the widower has not adapted to his new relationship.

Finally, one of the most telling red flags is the widower's difficulty in setting boundaries. When he cannot tell the difference between honouring the past and repeating it, or when he allows family or friends to dictate the new partner's role, the relationship becomes vulnerable to emotional imbalance. Family systems theory refers to this as a form of triangulation, where the widower becomes pulled between the expectations of the past and the needs of the present [26] [17]. In Donna's case, Chad broke this pattern by stepping in and setting a clear boundary with the football club. In contrast, James's lack of boundaries left Olivia feeling unheard, unprotected, and ultimately unsupported.

Recognising these red flags is essential for protecting emotional well-being and preventing the new partner from being consumed by someone else's history. These signs do not mean the widower is unkind or unloving; they are indicators that grief, nostalgia, and competing loyalties are shaping the relationship more powerfully than the present moment. As grief specialist J. William Worden emphasises, healing requires emotionally relocating the deceased, not erasing them but ensuring that their memory does not dominate the new relationship [4].

By recognising these patterns early, the new partner can better protect her identity, establish healthy boundaries, and engage in conversations that honour both the past and the present. Awareness is the first step toward building a relationship where the living is fully seen, valued, and loved, not for how well they replicate a memory, but for who they truly are.

Opening the Conversation

Talking to a widower about the pressure to step into the late wife's role can feel complicated, but approaching the conversation with care can prevent misunderstandings and strengthen your connection.

The aim is to express how certain situations affect you, without placing blame or criticising the past.

Focus on sharing your feelings rather than pointing out what he has done wrong. For example:

- "When I'm encouraged to follow the traditions your late wife created, I sometimes feel unsure of my own place in your life."
- "I notice I feel uncomfortable when comparisons are made, even unintentionally."

Framing the conversation around your emotional experience helps him understand what you're navigating, while keeping the discussion grounded and respectful.

Be specific about what feels difficult. You might say:

- "When your family suggests I host Christmas the way she did, I feel pressured to become someone I'm not."
- "When I'm asked to wear or use her belongings, I feel like I'm stepping into a role that isn't mine."

Clear examples help him see the pattern without feeling attacked.

Invite him to work with you on solutions. Questions such as:

- "How can we create new traditions that feel right for both of us?"
- "What boundaries can we set together so expectations from others don't impact our relationship?"

This creates a sense of teamwork rather than conflict.

Acknowledge his grief gently, while affirming your own needs. You may say:

- "I respect the love you shared, and I also want to feel valued for who I am now."
- "I'm not asking you to forget her, but I need space to be myself in our relationship."

Finally, reassure him that these conversations are about building a healthier future together, not erasing the past. Ending with a grounding statement can help bring the conversation back to connection:

- "I care about us, and talking about this helps me feel closer to you."

What to Remember

When a new relationship becomes a re-creation of the old, everyone loses. A loving partnership should make space for each person's individuality, not shape one partner into a placeholder for the past. Grief must be honoured, but not at the expense of someone else's identity.

Chapter 23 - Navigating The Late Wife Stories

"I thought my mind would explode if I had to listen to one more late wife story on an occasion special to us."

"I wanted to scream 'that's not my name' but politely nodded instead".

"I didn't like hearing repeated stories of how and when they met; I wanted to talk about how and when we met".

In this chapter, we explore the emotional complexities that surface when friends and family frequently reminisce about the widower's late wife in front of his new partner. These moments might come as shared stories, old photo albums, or casual comments that bring the past into the present. While the intention is often innocent, an effort to keep her memory alive, these situations can leave the new partner feeling pressured, uncomfortable, or quietly invisible. It can feel as though she is standing beside a love story she was never part of, yet constantly measured against.

Through case studies and professional insights, this chapter offers guidance on how to navigate these moments with compassion and clarity, how to set gentle boundaries, and how to honour the past without losing yourself in it. The aim is to help create a space where the memory of someone lost can coexist with the reality of someone new, without either woman being diminished in the process.

Case Study - Donna's Story

Donna had been in a relationship with her widower partner for 18 months when they planned a holiday to meet his family for the first time. Her partner had been estranged from them for years, only reconnecting after his late wife's passing. Donna felt a mix of excitement and nervous anticipation, having spoken to some relatives on the phone, but nothing could have prepared her for the dynamics she was about to encounter.

On the very first evening, her partner accidentally called her by his late wife's name, creating a heavy and immediate awkwardness. From that moment, Donna felt as though she were stepping into someone else's story rather than sharing her own with the family.

Throughout the trip, the family seemed to orbit the late wife's memory. They showed Donna places tied to the past, shared countless stories, and rifled through old photographs, leaving Donna on the periphery of every conversation. She tried to participate, but often felt invisible, unsure how to respond to recollections of a woman she had never known. Her own milestones, such as her birthday, went unnoticed except for a small gesture from her partner's sister, which highlighted just how absent she felt in this world that still seemed designed around someone else.

Donna was called by his late wife's name by other members of the family, though unintentional, added a sharp sting each time. Donna's excitement for connection and belonging began to shift into discomfort and a sense of exclusion. Feeling overwhelmed and emotionally isolated, she decided to visit a friend nearby for a few days, seeking respite from the constant reminders of the past.

Upon her return, her partner privately proposed, asking her to keep it secret until they had chosen a ring. For a moment, Donna allowed herself to hope that love might bridge the gap between her and the weight of his history. Yet, in retrospect, she recognised how much she had longed to feel valued in that family and how love sometimes blinded her to the reality of her emotional loneliness within his world.

Ultimately, the engagement never materialised publicly. No ring was ever chosen, and the relationship, strained by unacknowledged grief and persistent comparisons to the past, ended a year after the private proposal.

Case Study - Gertrude and Simon

Gertrude had spent many years healing from a toxic and violent marriage. She had worked hard to rediscover her sense of self, rebuild her confidence, and learn to trust again. When she cautiously opened her heart to Simon, a widower, it felt like a new beginning. Though hesitant at first, she slowly fell in love with him and was eager to meet the people who were important in his life.

Simon decided to host a large BBQ at his home, inviting nearly fifty guests, including his family, friends, and members of his late wife Lisa's family. Gertrude arrived full of hope but tinged with anxiety, unsure how she would be received.

From the moment introductions began, Gertrude noticed a pattern that made her stomach tighten. Many guests immediately referenced Lisa, often in ways that subtly compared her to the late wife: "Oh, Lisa would have loved you," "Lisa was such a great cook," "Lisa worshipped Simon," and "Simon will never love anyone the same way he loved Lisa." Others recounted endless stories of Simon's life with Lisa, and some questioned privately but loud enough for Gertrude to hear, whether he had "moved on too soon."

Despite being surrounded by friendly faces, Gertrude felt invisible. The focus on Lisa left her feeling like an outsider in what should have been a celebration of her new relationship. She longed for conversation about her experiences, her interests, and her bond with Simon, but found herself sidelined by constant reminders of a woman she had never met.

Turning to her own friends and family who had attended for support, Gertrude found temporary refuge. They listened, offered comfort, and allowed her to breathe amid the relentless comparisons and stories. But once she returned to Simon, the overwhelming pressure resurfaced. By the time the last guest departed, Gertrude was emotionally spent. She cried quietly, unable to fully articulate her feelings to Simon beyond saying that she felt overwhelmed.

Later, alone in the shower, she reflected on the experience. Why were people so intent on sharing Lisa's memories with her instead of taking the time to know her and honour the new relationship she was building with Simon? The intensity of the evening forced Gertrude to confront a painful truth: she felt like a bystander in her own life, overshadowed by the presence of someone who no longer existed. The experience left a lasting impression, highlighting the subtle yet profound ways that unresolved grief and the weight of memory can intrude on the emotional space of a new partner.

Recognising the Red Flags

Though Donna and Gertrude come from different backgrounds, Donna stepping into a relationship with a partner newly reconnected with his family, and Gertrude rebuilding trust after surviving a toxic marriage, they shared a common emotional struggle: feeling overshadowed by the memory of the late wife. Both women were introduced to circles where the late wife's memory dominated conversation, leading to feelings of invisibility and isolation.

In Donna's case, her partner and family members' repeated slips calling her by his late wife's name deepened the sense of being unseen. For Gertrude, the constant stories and guests' private doubts magnified the loneliness she had feared. Though the circumstances differ, both stories highlight the emotional toll of being asked to honour the late wife before truly being known for themselves. It's important to note that friends and family often believe sharing stories of the late wife helps welcome the new partner, but instead, it can create painful comparisons and reinforce a sense that the new partner may never fully belong.

The emotional experiences described by Donna and Gertrude reflect a common but often unspoken challenge faced by those who enter relationships with widowers: the ongoing presence of the deceased spouse within the social and emotional architecture of the widower's life. Psychologists and grief counsellors have long noted that while grief evolves, the way it is expressed, particularly in family and social circles, can either integrate a new partner or exclude her, even unintentionally [4] [26].

Attachment Theory plays a significant role in understanding these dynamics [29]. A widower's family and friends may cling to the memory of his late wife as a means of maintaining emotional security and preserving past identities [29]. In both Donna's and Gertrude's cases, the families unintentionally "froze" the late wife's place in the system, treating her memory not as a tribute but as a standard against which the new partner was measured. This can be emotionally damaging, creating what Pauline Boss describes as *ambiguous loss,* where the late wife is physically absent but psychologically omnipresent, complicating the new partner's ability to find her place [9].

From a grief counselling perspective, this issue is further compounded when the widower has not fully integrated the loss and instead externalises unresolved grief through ongoing symbolic gestures (such as mentioning the late wife frequently or mixing up names). These "slips" are not always about memory but about emotional placement, revealing that the new partner may be subconsciously compared to the late wife [3].

Furthermore, boundaries are often blurred in grieving families and social circles. When a new partner like Donna or Gertrude enters a tightly held circle of grief, her needs and identity can be quietly sidelined. The repeated failure to acknowledge relational milestones, misnaming, or centring conversations around the late wife are symptoms of a systemic grief pattern where the deceased wife is still treated as emotionally central, leaving no room for the new partner to be seen as a valid, equal presence.

While some families might believe they are honouring the past by inviting the new partner into those shared memories, they often fail to recognise how this can perpetuate emotional exclusion. New partners should be included not as substitutes but as distinct individuals. When this fails to happen, as with Donna's and Gertrude's cases, it can lead to resentment, confusion, and emotional exhaustion, as the new partner is asked to step into a script not written for her.

Opening the Conversation

When family and friends frequently share stories or memories of the late wife, a new partner can feel overlooked, compared, or invisible. Addressing these situations openly can help create a balance between honouring the past and nurturing the new relationship.

Acknowledge your feelings, begin by expressing your experience without placing blame:

- "I feel left out when conversations focus only on memories of [insert Late wife's name]."
- "I feel invisible when everyone talks about a past I wasn't part of."
- "I feel uncomfortable when I'm expected to react or participate in stories about [insert late wife's name] as I didn't know her and don't know what to say"

Invite collaboration. Frame your concerns as a shared problem rather than a criticism:

- "How can we talk about the past in a way that helps me feel included, not compared?"
- "Would it help if we agreed on when and how stories about [Insert late wife's name] are shared?"
- "I really enjoy hearing about your memories of [insert late wife's name], but sometimes I feel a little left out. Could we share some new memories about us, too?"
- "I'd love to hear about your memories at another time; right now, I want to focus on getting to know you."

Set gentle boundaries. Clarify what feels comfortable for you and what doesn't:

- "I'm happy to listen to stories occasionally, but I need to be able to join the conversation as myself."

- "It helps me when my thoughts and experiences are also acknowledged, not overshadowed by the past."

- "I understand you loved [insert late wife's name], but I'm learning to find my own way. I'd appreciate support for what I bring to the relationship."

- "I want to contribute in my own way, not be measured against someone else."

- "I value [insert late wife's name] memory, but I'd like to make decisions as a couple rather than only following past examples."

Encourage your partner's support because he can play an important role in mediating these interactions:

- "It helps when you redirect conversations if they become overwhelming for me."

- "Your reassurance and recognition of my presence make it easier for me to engage with your family and friends."

By acknowledging feelings, inviting collaboration, setting boundaries, and leaning on your partner's support, new partners can navigate conversations about the late wife while maintaining their sense of self and supporting a healthy, present-focused relationship.

What to Remember

The lesson is that remembrance and reinvention must be balanced; a loving future cannot fully emerge when it is built in the shadow of the past. Widowers, and those close to them, must create intentional space for the new partner to feel seen, valued, and actively included, not just as a comforting presence, but as an equal co-author of the next chapter.

Chapter 24 - The Late Wife's Friend who Cast Shadows

"I sometimes wondered if my partner's late wife's best friend was trying to get rid of me."

"There were many times that I felt overshadowed by her presence and often would find myself making excuses to not be around her."

"I thought that she was actively trying to destroy my relationship."

In this chapter, we will explore how the presence and influence of the late wife's best friend or other close confidantes can sometimes be unhealthy and can affect a widower's new relationship. This dynamic can be especially complex when the late wife's best friend openly shares her opinions, passes on the late wife's expressed wishes, or feels the need to remind the widower of shared memories and expectations without invitation.

We will discuss how this can create feelings of pressure, discomfort, or even resentment for the new partner, who may feel like she is competing with an idealised past or an ongoing loyalty to the late wife's social circle. We will discuss how some 'best friends' may see themselves as emotional gatekeepers to the widower's new relationship, the psychological impact on the new partner who may feel measured against a memory, and the delicate balance for the widower between honouring the past and creating a safe and balanced space for a new relationship.

We will also include case studies and expert commentary from grief counsellors, therapists, and relationship experts to help readers understand and navigate this emotionally charged situation.

Case Study - Julie, Mark, and Clara

Julie started dating Mark, a widower whose late wife, Anna, had passed away two years earlier. Early in their relationship, she noticed that Anna's best friend, Clara, was deeply involved in Mark's life. Clara frequently called or dropped by unannounced when Julie was staying over. She often spoke about what Anna "would have wanted and liked." She openly shared stories about Mark and Anna's marriage and even invited herself to Mark's family gatherings.

At times, Clara made subtle suggestions that Julie should behave more like Anna, who had been outgoing and confident, and implied that certain decisions should honour Anna's memory. Mark rarely challenged Clara's input and seemed to defer to her out of loyalty and guilt. Julie, having never been in a relationship with a widower before, was taken aback; in most relationships, she thought, it would be considered disrespectful to repeatedly reference a previous partner in this way.

Julie soon felt as though she had to gain Clara's approval to belong in Mark's life and began worrying constantly about Clara's next visit. Instead of focusing on building a future together, her attention was consumed by competing with the idealised memory of Anna that Clara reinforced. Over time, this dynamic eroded Julie's sense of security and left her feeling secondary in her relationship with Mark.

Julie tried to speak to Mark about her concerns. Mark acknowledged them but explained that he didn't want to upset Clara, insisting she was just being well-meaning and had been such a good friend to Anna. After some time, Julie realised that she was still feeling uneasy, unsupported and unable to establish healthy boundaries with Mark regarding Clara, Julie decided to end the relationship. She later learned that Mark had begun a relationship with Clara, a revelation that, in hindsight, helped explain the intensity of Clara's involvement and influence.

Case Study - Melissa, Gerry, and Lisa

Melissa had been in a committed relationship with Gerry for almost two years, and they had been living together for five months. Yet one steady source of strain was Lisa, the late wife's best friend. From the very beginning, Lisa maintained an unusually strong presence in Gerry's life. She often reminded people that she had known the late wife for decades and "knew the house like the back of her hand." Using a spare key Gerry had never asked for back, Lisa routinely let herself into their home without warning. Lisa would rearrange furniture "back to the way her best friend liked it", and without being asked, she cleaned and tidied the house according to how Gerry's late wife preferred things, reclaiming the space as if it were hers to manage.

Melissa soon began to feel like a visitor in her own home. While she was at work, Lisa would drop by with groceries she insisted Gerry enjoyed or cook meals from recipes his late wife used. More than once, Melissa walked in after a long day to find Lisa asleep on the couch, an unfinished glass of wine resting on the table. Gerry brushed off Melissa's discomfort, saying Lisa was "just trying to help," but the line between support and intrusion had blurred beyond recognition.

The most shocking moment came when Melissa found Lisa in Gerry's bedroom wearing Gerry's late wife's wedding dress. Lisa claimed she was "trying it on for sentimental reasons" and insisted that her friend would have approved, and then suggested that she should be given the wedding dress. The dress had been carefully stored away and was something Gerry wanted to give to his only daughter when she returned from overseas. Hearing that Lisa was wearing it felt like a profound violation of trust, memory, and private grief, yet he didn't speak up or ask for the key back.

Things escalated when Lisa let herself in unannounced again and noticed that her best friend's wedding photos and ashes had been moved out of the living area. Lisa took it upon herself to go through the cupboards and rooms to find the missing items and put them back in their original spots. What Lisa didn't know was that Gerry had quietly relocated these things to a more discreet place in the home and was waiting for his daughter to return before he scattered his late wife's ashes and gave her the photos.

Melissa returned home and thought that Gerry had moved the ashes back to the living area, unaware that

Lisa had let herself in again. Melissa, crying, asked Gerry if he felt ready for a relationship. The conversation became confusing and turned into their first argument. Only later did the truth surface: Lisa had moved her best friend back into the living area. When confronted, Lisa admitted it and defended her actions by saying, "I just couldn't stand to see her hidden away like that."

Lisa became passive-aggressive and her remarks continued to undermine Melissa, joking that Melissa "wasn't much of a cook," or that "Gerry always liked things done a certain way." Though subtle, these comments chipped away at Melissa's confidence and sense of place in her relationship. She began to feel not only overshadowed by the memory of his late wife but displaced by a woman who seemed determined to protect a past identity that no longer fit the present.

Melissa loved Gerry, but the constant intrusion and emotional manipulation, and Gerry's reluctance to set boundaries, left her questioning whether there was truly space for her in his life. Her needs were repeatedly dismissed in the name of loyalty to the deceased, and over time, the emotional cost became too heavy to carry, and she walked away.

Recognising the Red Flags

Julie and Melissa's experiences show how a widower's late wife's close friends can subtly or overtly shape a new relationship, often in ways that feel controlling or intrusive. In both cases, the best friends, Clara and Lisa, acted as "emotional gatekeepers," reinforcing the memory of the deceased and making it difficult for the new partner to feel fully present. For Julie, the influence was quiet but persistent. Clara's closeness to Anna's memory created an unspoken standard, and Julie found herself constantly aware of being measured against someone she could never replace. Melissa's experience was far more invasive. Lisa entered the home uninvited, rearranged spaces, and even wore the late wife's wedding dress, leaving Melissa feeling like a guest in her own life.

These experiences highlight several clear red flags in relationships with widowers. One is the lack of clear boundaries with the late wife's friends or family, allowing the past to take precedence over the present. Another is ongoing comparison to the deceased, which can foster feelings of inadequacy, anxiety, and self-doubt. A third is physical or ritual intrusion into the household, which undermines autonomy, emotional safety, and the new partner's sense of belonging. Finally, the prioritisation of loyalty to the deceased over the new partner can leave her feeling overshadowed and emotionally secondary, creating a dynamic where she struggles to have her identity and needs recognised.

Clinical psychologists and grief specialists describe these patterns as part of the "continuing bonds" people maintain with those who have passed. These bonds can be healthy when expressed through respectful memory or shared rituals, but become harmful when others use them to set the terms of the widower's current life [30][4][17]. Living under constant comparison can erode self-esteem, create frustration, and even contribute to stress-related health issues over time [20]. Without clear boundaries, the influence of people close to the late wife can undermine trust, intimacy, and emotional safety [8].

Therapists emphasise that widowers must recognise these dynamics and actively create space for the present. Healthy relationships require mutual consent to form new memories, rituals, and emotional norms, rather than continuing to live in a past that no longer fits [17][9]. Encouraging open dialogue, clarifying where remembrance ends and the present begins, and seeking support through therapy or mediation can help ensure the relationship is shaped by the living, rather than dominated by the memory of someone who has gone [8][9][4].

Opening the Conversation

When your partner's late wife's friends overstep, gentle but honest conversations can help restore balance. These conversation starters give readers simple, respectful ways to express their feelings and set boundaries with both the widower and the friend involved.

When discussing boundary issues with your partner, the goal is to be clear, calm, and anchored in your own emotional experience rather than blame. Here are examples of gentle, direct ways to open the conversation:

- "I know [Insert friend's name] has been a big part of your life, but sometimes her involvement makes me feel pushed aside. I'd like us to set boundaries that protect what we're creating."
- "When I'm compared to [Insert the late wife's name], even subtly, it impacts how safe I feel. I need your support in setting boundaries around that."
- "I'm not asking you to choose between the past and the present, but I do need our relationship to have its own space. Can we agree on a few boundaries together?"

- "I want us to build something of our own. What do you think would help protect our relationship from outside pressure?"

When speaking directly to the friend who is overstepping, the aim is to remain respectful while asserting your emotional boundaries. These conversation starters can help:

- "I respect the bond you had with [Insert the late wife's name]. I'd like to share how some things are affecting me so we can move forward respectfully."
- "When I'm compared to [Insert the late wife's name], it becomes hard for me to feel comfortable. Could we avoid those comparisons?"
- "I know you want to support him, and so do I. How can we both do that without stepping on each other's space?"
- "I'm not trying to replace [Insert the late wife's name], but I do need space to build my own connection here."

Opening these conversations can feel uncomfortable, especially when grief, loyalty, and long-standing friendships are involved. But clear, compassionate communication gives the new partner a voice and helps the widower recognise where old patterns may be unintentionally harming the present.

Setting boundaries is not a rejection of the past; it is an invitation to create a healthier, more balanced future. When handled with honesty and respect, these conversations can strengthen the relationship rather than threaten it, allowing everyone involved to move forward with greater clarity and emotional safety.

What to Remember

When a widower does not establish clear emotional or physical boundaries with people closely connected to his late wife, especially her best friends or long-term confidantes, it can create an unhealthy triangle that leaves the new partner feeling sidelined.

Dear Me

I didn't realise how much it would cost me to keep quiet. I thought staying patient and accommodating would help things flow more naturally. I thought smiling through discomfort meant I was being mature, understanding, and compassionate. But slowly, quietly, I began losing pieces of myself in places I never expected to.

I walked into situations I didn't know how to read and listened to opinions delivered as obligations, the stories that centred on a past I wasn't part of. I didn't see them for what they were at the time: red flags disguised as loyalty, grief, or "good intentions." I just kept trying to be gracious, hoping that kindness would create space for me in a life that already felt crowded.

There were moments I wanted to speak up but didn't know how. Moments where something felt wrong, but I convinced myself it would settle. I told myself to be understanding; everyone was grieving, everyone was adjusting, but I never stopped to ask why I was the only one adjusting to everyone else.

And when someone crossed a line, stepped into the relationship, or positioned themselves as a gatekeeper to it, I tried to make sense of it quietly, internally. I tried to give the benefit of the doubt, even when doubt was all I had left. I didn't know that protecting myself wasn't selfish; it was necessary. I didn't know that silence can be damaging, and not a gesture of peace.

Now I see it clearly: I wasn't weak. I was navigating a world no one prepared me for, a world where the past is still alive in other people. I did the best that I could with the knowledge I had at the time. I didn't fail for not recognising the red flags, I learned to see them by living through them.

So, I forgive myself for staying quiet when I felt uneasy, for making myself small to keep harmony, for trying to belong in a space that didn't know how to make room for me. I thought patience would eventually become partnership. I thought understanding would turn into safety and that kindness would be enough.

I now know that I deserve to be in a relationship where I don't have to compete with memories or manage other people's grief. I deserve a partner who protects my place beside him, not one who leaves me to navigate outsiders alone. I deserve to feel chosen, supported, and seen.

So, this is what I promise myself: I will never again shrink myself for the comfort of others. I will never again dismiss my own intuition to avoid confrontation. And I will never again let anyone, friend, family, or ghost of the past, define my worth or my place in a relationship.

With love,
Me

Part 4 – The Painful End.

This part of the book is for the women who've asked themselves the hard questions:

Is he truly ready to love someone new, or am I just filling the space she left behind?

Why do I feel lonelier beside him than I ever did alone?

Is this grief... or something more damaging?

From the outside, loving a widower can seem noble, romantic, even healing. We're often told that grief is love with nowhere to go, and that with enough compassion, understanding, and patience, a new love can bloom in its shadow. But what most people don't see are the hidden emotional costs. They don't witness the quiet ache of being compared to someone who's no longer here. They don't hear the silence after a sudden emotional withdrawal or the confusion that comes when grief is used to justify emotional unavailability, blame, or even to manipulate.

In the chapters that follow, we'll explore the mental and emotional toll this kind of relationship can take, especially when it's unbalanced, one-sided, or grounded in unresolved grief. We'll look at the subtle shift from mourning to manipulation, and how to recognise when compassion is being exploited.

You'll find guidance on:

- What to do if the relationship isn't strong enough to last.
- How to cope if a widower ends things abruptly.
- How to end the relationship yourself, with dignity and clarity.
- And most importantly, how to heal and move forward with your self-worth intact

This isn't just about loss. It's about rediscovery. Because even when a relationship doesn't last, your love wasn't wasted; it was real.

Chapter 25 –Scorched by the Widowers' Fire

"I felt selfish every time I wanted to be seen; I wanted him to look at me the same way that he did when we met."

"I lost my spark. His grief was allowed. My hurt felt shameful."

"He swept me off my feet and then dumped me a week after what would have been his wedding anniversary with his late wife."

In this chapter, we will speak honestly about the uncomfortable truth that there are men who, knowingly or unknowingly, use the intimacy, goodwill, and love of a new partner to help manage their grief or to distract themselves from it.

As we have explored, unresolved grief can prevent a widower from fully committing to new love. The emotional toll of living in someone else's shadow is rarely spoken of in society. Many women in relationships with unhealed widowers face challenges that would be unacceptable and unimaginable in "typical" relationship terms.

The *Widower's Fire* is real. It is intense, consuming, and can be as disorienting as it is alluring. One of the hardest truths women often face is the fact that the *Widower's Fire* is more about the widower's need for healing through intimacy than about emotional attachment or love. Women caught in this fire may feel exhilaration and fear, joy and confusion, often at the same time.

The *Widower's Fire* can cast a powerful light, one that exposes emotional truths, hidden patterns, and unhealed wounds that might otherwise stay buried. Recognising this fire is not about judgment; it is about awareness.

We must acknowledge the experiences of women who were scorched by the *Widowers Fire*, women who felt that their hearts, their time, and sometimes even their bodies were used as a distraction from grief.

Case Study - Ella and Daniel

Ella met Daniel in a bookshop. He was warm, attentive, and carried a quiet sadness that made her want to understand him. Within weeks, he was texting every morning, leaving small gestures of affection, and speaking with a vulnerability that made Ella feel chosen. The pace was intense and passionate, and she was quickly swept into the connection.

As the anniversary of his late wife's death approached, everything changed. Daniel became withdrawn and unresponsive. Ella, worried, called around to Daniels house to check on him, but he stepped outside rather than inviting her in. He explained that his late wife's family was staying with him and mentioned the memorial service that had taken place the week before. He ended the conversation before she could speak.

Ella left feeling dismissed and confused. The closeness she believed they were building disappeared without warning. Weeks later, Daniel reached out again. When Ella expressed how hurt she felt, how used and invisible she had been, he brushed her off, insisting she didn't understand grief.

In that moment, she finally saw the pattern: the intensity of their early connection was driven by Daniel's unresolved grief, not emotional readiness. His need for closeness had filled the emptiness grief left behind, but it never made room for her. Realising this, Ella chose to end the relationship. The pain came not only from losing Daniel, but from recognising she had stepped into a space where she was never going to be fully seen or genuinely loved.

Case Study - Amy and Warren

Amy dated Warren for eight months. At first, she was swept away by his attentiveness, the way he seemed to want to make every moment meaningful. But gradually, the spark that had drawn her in became a flicker. Warren would pull back without explanation, retreating into silence that seemed to come out of nowhere. She asked him if he was okay and if their relationship was okay. He said he was not trying to be cruel; he said he was grieving, but his admission left Amy confused and anxious.

The passion she had mistaken for love revealed itself as his reaction to loss. Amy began to understand that what she had felt at the beginning was never fully about her; it was about Warren. It was one of the hardest lessons she had to learn: the early passion, she realised, was a distraction from his grief. Warren ended the relationship without discussion.

Case Study - Amelia and Thomas

Thomas met Amelia ten months after his late wife's death. Their relationship began with intense passion, and after five months of dating, they decided to move in together. Amelia sold her home and invested in Thomas's house, excited that they were building a shared future.

At first, everything seemed wonderful, but within a few months, Amelia noticed troubling patterns. Thomas had become increasingly withdrawn, and his late wife's belongings remained in every cupboard and drawer. A large shelf, essentially a shrine, was still filled with photos and mementos of his late wife, and he had even added new items. Amelia had to keep her clothes and personal belongings in a spare room because Thomas insisted that he wasn't ready to pack away his late wife's belongings, despite having previously promised he would.

Amelia also noticed that the passion and attention that had marked the early months of their relationship were fading. Compliments became rare, replaced by subtle and sometimes overt comparisons to his late wife. Thomas would remark on how she could improve in ways his late wife supposedly would have excelled, how she kept the house, handled conversations, or responded to him. When Amelia tried to express her feelings about the growing distance, Thomas would shut down, remaining silent for days.

Amelia began to feel as though she was there only to fill a void for Thomas, rather than being loved and appreciated as a partner. This led to mounting anxiety, sleepless nights, and repeated self-doubt. Her sense of self-worth eroded; she increasingly felt like a placeholder rather than an equal in the relationship. Despite her efforts to create new memories and bond with Thomas, he remained emotionally anchored in the past. The intensity and passion that had drawn her in at the beginning were gone, leaving Amelia hurt and unfulfilled.

Ultimately, Amelia recognised that Thomas could not meet her emotional needs or stay fully present in their relationship. Realising she deserved to be seen, loved, and valued as herself, she made the difficult decision to get a lawyer and move out.

Case Study - Rachel and David

David had been widowed for three years, and Rachel was his third partner since the passing of his late wife. According to David, his previous relationships ended because his partners didn't understand his grief and were insensitive to his need to mourn.

Rachel's relationship with David began like a whirlwind, full of passion, laughter, and daily communication through calls and messages. At first, Rachel felt she had found "the one." After nearly a year together, Rachel began to see a disturbing pattern: during anniversaries and other dates tied to his life with his late wife, David would withdraw, sometimes not answering her messages or calls for days or even weeks.

When Rachel finally worked up the courage to share how this made her feel, David deflected, insisting that he needed space to grieve, accused her of being selfish and insensitive, and then abruptly ended the relationship. Rachel found herself questioning her own perceptions, feeling sad and confused, as the man she had fallen for seemed to transform into someone emotionally unavailable.

For Rachel, the emotional neglect created isolation and confusion. She felt used, which was impacted by the psychological toll of being with an unhealed widower and compounded by the heartbreak of rejection. Ultimately, Rachel focused on her own healing and self-care. Meanwhile, David moved on to his fourth partner since his late wife's death.

Widowers Fire – The Uncomfortable Truth

Across the case studies, a clear and confronting pattern emerges: the intensity that draws women into these relationships is often less about genuine emotional connection and more about the widower's unresolved grief. The *Widower's Fire* is consuming, seductive, and deeply disorienting. It promises intimacy, passion, and emotional closeness, yet it is fuelled by absence, longing, and a need to reclaim vitality after loss. For the women who step into this fire, the experience can feel exhilarating one moment and devastating the next.

Ella and Daniel's story captures both the allure and the cost. Their connection was immediate and tender, marked by constant attention and emotional openness that made Ella feel chosen and deeply seen. Yet as the anniversary of his late wife's death approached, Daniel withdrew, ignored her calls, and left her reaching for a closeness that was never truly available to her. Ella's heartbreak came not only from the loss of the relationship but from recognising that the intensity she believed reflected love was, for him, a distraction from grief rather than a commitment to her.

Amy and Warren followed a similar emotional pattern. Amy was swept up in charm, attentiveness, and passion, only to be met with sudden withdrawal as Warren retreated into his grief without warning. The emotional highs were mirrored by abrupt lows, leaving Amy anxious, destabilised, and questioning whether she was ever loved for who she was, or simply for how effectively she filled the space left by his loss.

The longer-term consequences of unresolved grief are evident in the experiences of Amelia and Thomas, and

Rachel and David. Amelia endured subtle but persistent comparisons to Thomas's late wife, constant reminders that her presence was secondary, and the slow erosion of her sense of self. Sleepless nights, mounting anxiety, and relentless self-doubt became her daily reality. Rachel experienced repeated cycles of emotional withdrawal around anniversaries, followed by abrupt rejection. Both women were left emotionally scorched, carrying the weight of love that had never fully belonged to them.

Psychologists note that grief can heighten emotional responsiveness, intensifying attachment and early expressions of passion [9][29]. But understanding why this happens offers little comfort to the women who are hurt by it. Much of what is used to explain the *Widower's Fire* exists only in fragments: a paragraph in grief research, a brief mention in attachment theory, a small inclusion in discussions of bereavement and neurochemistry. There is no body of work devoted to examining the psychological damage experienced by women who become emotionally, physically, and financially invested in relationships with unhealed widowers. The research helps us understand the widower's inner world, but it rarely asks what happens to the woman standing beside him.

This absence matters. Entire fields of research examine male behaviours that harm women: violence, coercive control, narcissism, emotional abuse, financial exploitation, sexual entitlement, and the use of women's bodies for gratification. Yet there is little scrutiny of men who use women's emotional labour, intimacy, and attachment as a means of self-soothing, regulation, and distraction from grief. This form of harm is quieter, easier to excuse, and far more likely to be reframed as understandable rather than acknowledged as damaging.

Professionals note that neurochemically, surges of intimacy can temporarily soothe loneliness and longing, creating cycles of connection and withdrawal that destabilise a partner's sense of love and safety [32]. What is rarely discussed is the cost to the woman who falls in love, invests emotionally, physically, and often financially, only to be discarded once the fire cools. The *Widower's Fire* damages self-esteem, confidence, trust, family connections, and social stability. Many women experience lasting financial and emotional fallout after relationships that collapse without warning.

Women scorched by the *Widower's Fire* often struggle to be heard or believed. They are told to be more understanding, reminded that "he moved on too soon," or asked to excuse behaviour that would be unacceptable in any other relationship. Sympathy is reserved for the widower, who is seen as tragic and fragile, while the woman's pain is minimised, explained away, or quietly dismissed.

Clinicians describe this pattern as a grief-driven rebound, where the desire for closeness emerges rapidly but does not reflect a stable or reciprocal bond [32]. In other contexts, using another person's body and emotional availability to heal would be met with criticism and concern. Here, it is often rationalised. Without resolution of past grief, the *Widower's Fire* burns unpredictably, leaving the partner emotionally battered in its aftermath.

When grief remains unresolved, emotional availability becomes anchored in the past, forcing new partners to navigate disappointment, self-doubt, and the psychological toll of loving someone who is not fully present [8]. The early passion of the *Widower's Fire* masks emotional unavailability, igniting quickly but struggling to sustain healthy intimacy. Many women internalise the confusion, turning the blame inward and questioning their own worth, patience, or capacity to love.

The *Widower's Fire* is not simply attraction or sexual chemistry; it is a grief-driven psychological response. For some widowers, a new relationship becomes a way of easing emptiness and emotional pain rather than a fully conscious choice. While affection may be genuine, it is often entwined with the projection of unmet emotional needs, leaving the partner carrying feelings that were never hers to bear [33]. As Dr Susan J. Elliott notes, this dynamic can quietly erode self-esteem and generate anxiety, leaving the partner feeling perpetually compared, secondary, or invisible [8].

Relationships grounded in mutual respect, emotional presence, and shared meaning are only possible when grief is acknowledged but no longer allowed to dominate the emotional landscape [3][8]. For the women who step into these relationships, the *Widower's Fire* does not simply fade. It often leaves hearts bruised, identities shaken, and lives unsettled, a reminder that love lived in the shadow of a ghost can burn down the home it was never meant to inhabit.

What to Remember

The *Widower's Fire* is an intense, often intoxicating rush, fuelled more by unresolved grief than by present love. It can feel like a deep, immediate bond, yet beneath the intensity lies emotional distance, sudden withdrawal, and a heart left scorched. The fire ignites quickly, consuming attention, affection, and trust, leaving the partner to navigate confusion, self-doubt, and the upheaval of her life. The *Widower's Fire* may burn bright, but for those caught in it, the ashes are theirs to carry.

Chapter 26 – Is it Grief or Manipulation

"He would ghost me on the anniversary dates he shared with his late

wife, and it felt like he went out of his way to remind me that I'm not her."

"He would get moody and angry at certain times of the year. I never knew what to say or do that would help him."

"He got up in my face and told me that I'm being insensitive and then slammed the door as he left the room".

Sometimes, it's hard to tell where grief ends, and manipulation begins, especially when dating a widower who hasn't fully faced his loss. In the beginning, it may feel caring to soften your boundaries, to absorb his pain, to be endlessly patient, but patterns soon emerge. You may start to notice that his grief isn't just sorrow; it's being used as a shield, a weapon, or a way to control, deflect, or avoid accountability [49] [47].

Grief is real, complex, and unique to every individual. But when it leaves you anxious, unseen, or blamed consistently, it stops being just mourning; it becomes manipulation.

This chapter is for the women who find themselves caught in this cycle: women whose empathy and care are exploited, whose emotional labour is extracted while the widower remains anchored in the past [54] [48].

The consequences are concrete. Emotional manipulation masquerading as grief erodes self-esteem, undermines confidence, strains friendships, destabilises trust, and can have financial or social repercussions [50] [51]. Unlike overt forms of male harm, such as domestic abuse, sexual coercion, or financial exploitation, this type of manipulation is subtle, socially excused, and under-researched. Yet its impact is real, measurable, and lasting [52] [57].

Grief itself is natural; manipulation is deliberate. Widowers who weaponise their loss do more than struggle; they use grief to extract emotional labour, enforce compliance, and control their partner, leaving women to navigate the fallout alone.

Psychological research demonstrates that emotional manipulation has huge consequences, even without physical violence. It can increase anxiety and depression, disrupt sleep, and reduce cognitive clarity [48] [50].

Society often gives this behaviour a pass. Statements like "he's been through so much" or "you should be more understanding of his grief" normalise conduct that would otherwise be recognised as coercive control or psychological abuse [47] [56]. The effects rarely stay contained within the relationship. Trust falters, connections with friends and family are tested, social worlds grow smaller, and financial stability can be unsettled when time, care, and resources are devoted to a relationship that cannot meet them in return [53][54].

Clinicians and abuse researchers describe this manipulation as a pattern: gaslighting, blame-shifting, emotional withdrawal, and destabilising swings between intensity and absence [52][58]. Women in these relationships speak of chronic self-doubt, anxiety, and a quiet erosion of confidence. Gradually, they stop trusting their own perceptions, internalising blame and learning to silence themselves in order to keep the peace [55][49]. When care flows in only one direction, emotional exhaustion and relational collapse predictably follow [53][57].

Even seemingly small behaviours, being compared unfavourably to the deceased spouse, having plans cancelled without warning, or having emotional needs ignored, constitute ongoing manipulation [49][54]. Over time, these behaviours create patterns where women feel powerless, internalising blame while the widower's grief is always prioritised [47].

Unlike other male challenges, this harm is quiet, often invisible, and rarely examined. But the fallout is severe. Women may experience heightened anxiety, depression, post-traumatic stress symptoms, and difficulty trusting future partners [50]. Financial consequences can also occur when resources, time, attention, and money are invested in a relationship controlled through emotional leverage [56].

This is not "just grief." It is manipulation dressed in mourning, with tangible, long-term impacts. Until the psychological, relational, and material consequences of this dynamic are acknowledged, studied, and understood, women will continue to bear its hidden cost. Their experiences demand recognition. And their survival strategies, setting boundaries, seeking therapy, and reclaiming autonomy, are not weaknesses; they are acts of courage [51] [47].

Case Study: Sophie and Daniel

Daniel lost his wife, Claire, five years ago. Early in the relationship, Sophie noticed red flags: every conversation returned to his grief, loneliness, or comparisons to his late wife. When Sophie expressed her needs, Daniel replied, "Claire would have been more understanding." He refused couples counselling, claimed he didn't need help, and shamed Sophie for feeling hurt.

Over time, his grief became a pattern of manipulation: looping conversations back to his loss, blaming Sophie for "insensitivity," and withholding emotional availability. Sophie felt constantly destabilised, anxious, and unsure if her love or her very presence mattered, ultimately recognising that she was being used as an emotional placeholder.

Case Study: Joanne and Peter

Peter had been widowed for eight years when he began dating Joanne. In the early stages, he seemed sensitive and attentive, but over time, his behaviour shifted. He idealised his late wife while subtly criticising Joanne, comparing her to the woman he had lost.

Peter refused to celebrate Joanne's milestones, dismissed her opinions, and imposed traditional household roles, framing them as "normal" because that's what he had been used to. When Joanne tried to set boundaries or express her feelings, Peter accused her of jealousy or cruelty, using his grief to justify controlling behaviour.

Eventually, Joanne recognised the manipulation. Peter's anger confirmed what she had feared: she could never meet his emotional needs, nor could she compete with a memory. She left, reclaiming her self-worth and emotional safety.

Case Study: Emma and David

Emma dated David three years after his wife, Caroline, passed away. At first, she was moved by his stories of loyalty and grief. But soon, his sorrow dominated daily life: he cancelled important plans without explanation, used Caroline as a standard against which Emma was constantly measured, and shamed her for wanting connection.

When Emma suggested therapy, David refused, claiming Caroline "would never have asked him to change." Emma felt invisible, anxious, and emotionally drained. While David's grief was real, the impact on Emma was significant: her needs were sidelined, her voice muted, and her well-being compromised. Emma's decision to step back was an act of self-preservation, not a rejection of his grief.

A Red Flag for Manipulation

A key warning sign is when grief becomes an excuse for ongoing unhealthy behaviour. Does he repeatedly cancel plans at the last minute? Expect you to absorb his mood swings without question? Dismiss your feelings as "insensitive" or "selfish"? Does he consistently frame his grief as justification for emotional distance or unpredictability?

Another sign is using his late spouse as a tool to avoid accountability. Phrases such as "She would have understood" or "You don't know how hard life is without her" are red flags. They signal that you are being positioned as a placeholder rather than a partner, and that your feelings are secondary to an idealised memory.

Healthy relationships require balance. Compassion for someone grieving is vital, but so is compassion for yourself. If grief is wielded as a wall, or worse, a tool to control and silence, it's time to take stock. At first, you may question your own responses: Am I being supportive? Am I being manipulated? Recognising the difference is crucial.

Understanding the Effects of Manipulation

These case studies illustrate that grief affects widowers in very different ways. Some mourn while remaining present and accountable; others weaponise their grief to extract emotional labour, control partners, or avoid facing the present.

Professional research on grief, attachment, and personality explains the widower's pain, yet it rarely addresses the damage inflicted on their partners [4][9][29]. Emotional manipulation disguised as grief is subtle, socially excused, and understudied. Its consequences, battered self-esteem, eroded confidence, strained friendships, financial loss, and trust issues, are real, measurable, and long-lasting.

Grief-driven manipulation differs from other male behaviours. Unlike domestic abuse, sexual coercion, or narcissistic exploitation, it is quieter, harder to name, and often minimised. Women in these dynamics are frequently told to be understanding, patient, or compassionate, while the widower's behaviour is excused.

Clinicians describe this pattern as a grief-driven rebound, where closeness emerges rapidly but does not reflect a shared bond [32]. When grief remains unresolved, it can become a weapon, leaving partners emotionally battered. Experts note that unprocessed grief anchors emotional availability in the past, forcing new partners to navigate repeated disappointment, self-doubt, and ongoing psychological strain [8].

Grief vs Narcissism

Grief: Often self-focused at first, but softens over time. Includes guilt, sadness, and longing, yet leaves room to care for a new partner. Can improve with therapy and open communication [4][9].

Narcissism: Emotional focus stays rigidly on self, due to entitlement. Lacks empathy, uses blame, gaslighting, or silent treatment. Sees partners as extensions of self rather than equals [21].

The key difference: A grieving widower may be emotionally unavailable but wishes it were otherwise. A narcissist remains rigidly self-focused, often using grief as a shield for manipulation.

Checklist: Am I Supporting Grief—or Being Manipulated?

Reflect honestly on these questions. A few "yes" answers may be normal in a relationship still adjusting to loss, but if you see a consistent pattern, it's worth deeper reflection or professional guidance.

- Do I feel guilty asking for basic respect, attention, or affection?
- Does he use his late wife's memory to silence or dismiss my concerns?
- Do conversations about his grief ignore my feelings?
- Do I defend his behaviour to friends or family, even when hurt?
- Do holidays and milestones revolve around his grief, leaving little room for shared joy?
- Has he blamed me for being "insensitive" when I expressed needs?
- Am I giving more emotional support than I receive, with little hope of balance?

- Has his grief become a constant reason not to commit, define, or move forward?

Not every widower who struggles with grief is manipulative. Many are genuinely trying, even imperfectly, to heal and love again. But if his grief has become: a wall you can never cross, a weapon used to silence your feelings, or a story that always casts him as the victim and you as the problem, then it may be time to step back. Walking away doesn't mean you didn't care. It means you chose to care for yourself, too.

What to Remember

Grief can make love tender and complex, but it should never make you invisible, responsible for someone else's healing, or constantly depleted. True connection grows from mutual respect, emotional availability, and shared commitment. If grief becomes a shield for control, blame, or emotional distance, it is not your job to fix him. Protect your peace. Love should feel like a partnership, not a sacrifice.

Chapter 27 – When The Fire Turns to Ash

'I thought I had met the man of my dreams, but he ghosted me for a ghost."

"I feel used and stupid."

"He moved on, but I'm still heartbroken."

This chapter creates space to explore why some unhealed widowers end their relationships. The intention is not to criticise but to illuminate the emotional reality of unresolved grief. When a woman loves a widower, whose heart is still intertwined with his past, grief doesn't sit outside the relationship; it becomes part of its foundation. Many of these relationships begin with warmth, intensity, and a sense of possibility, yet end in ways that feel abrupt, disorienting, and painful.

While every story is different, a common thread emerges: the *Widowers Fire,* that passionate, urgent energy that initially feels like a deep connection, slowly burns out once the emotional relief it provided is no longer needed. What once felt like love begins to unravel because it was built upon grief rather than stability.

After a breakup, society tends to extend immediate empathy to the widower. Statements like, "He moved on too soon, he must be struggling", are quite common. However, far less consideration is given to the woman who steps into his life with an open heart. Often unknowingly, she becomes part of his recovery process, carrying a weight she never agreed to hold.

It is especially painful when a relationship ends around emotionally charged dates linked to his late wife. For the woman who is present and invested, the timing can feel bewildering and deeply hurtful. She may interpret the ending as a reflection of her own inadequacy instead of recognising it as a sign of his unresolved attachment.

When breakups happen suddenly and without meaningful conversation, they leave lasting emotional wounds. Many women describe questioning their worth or wondering whether they were truly seen or simply providing comfort during a moment of grief-driven vulnerability.

Several women have shared that during the breakup, the widower referenced his late wife as the reason he could not continue. He may say he is "not ready," or that he wants his life to remain as it was when "she died." While these words can be honest, they are often devastating to hear. They signal the extinguishing of the *Widower's Fire*, the closing of a chapter she believed held a future. She is left standing in the remains of a love that, in hindsight, was not fully available to her.

When the *Widower's Fire* fades, it rarely fades gently. It often burns the woman who loved him, leaving her holding both her own heartbreak and the emotional residue of his grief. Many women describe feeling confused, angry, or deeply sorrowful, grieving someone who is still alive. The psychological impact can linger for years, shaping self-trust and future relationships, and creating a fear of being compared to someone's past.

From a psychological and neurobiological perspective, the *Widower's Fire* is where grief collides with unmet emotional needs. Moments of intimacy, reassurance, and closeness can briefly soothe the brain's stress response, reigniting the very systems, dopamine and oxytocin, that underpin bonding and reward [34]. A new relationship can momentarily restore these pathways, creating an intense, almost instant attachment. But when connection is used more to dull emotional pain than to nurture real healing, the fire cannot sustain itself, and the partner is left navigating the burn.

This is where emotional intelligence becomes essential. Moving into a new relationship after loss requires self-awareness, willingness to seek support, and the capacity to distinguish between comfort-seeking and authentic readiness [35] [36]. Without these capacities, a widower may unintentionally use intimacy as a substitute for grief work. In those moments, closeness becomes a temporary balm, not a stable foundation.

For the woman involved, this dynamic can be profoundly damaging. She may feel emotionally abandoned once the widower withdraws. Her heart and body may have been part of his healing process, only for her to be left behind when the illusion of readiness fades. Emotional rejection after periods of intense intimacy activates the same neural pathways as physical pain [37]. She is not only grieving the loss of the relationship; she may also be grieving the loss of self-trust, safety, and the belief that love can be secure.

Understanding this dynamic does not excuse the hurt that may occur, but it helps make sense of how love and grief can become entangled in ways that feel deeply unfair.

The *Widower's Fire* is real, it burns brightly, offering warmth and connection for a time, but unless it is fuelled by genuine healing rather than emotional hunger, it cannot last. And when it goes out, the silence that follows can feel colder and more disorienting than the loneliness that came before.

Case Study: Emma and Daniel

Emma had fallen heavily for Daniel, a widower. Their relationship felt steady with dinners with Emma's friends, weekend getaways, and conversations about a shared future. A week before the anniversary of Daniel's late wife's passing, Emma noticed that Daniel had started wearing his wedding ring again, and he became quieter and seemed irritable; their usual messages grew sparse, plans they'd made for the weekend were suddenly "too much".

Three days before his old anniversary date, Daniel ended the relationship in a brief phone call. He told Emma, *"It's not fair to you. I can't give you what you deserve.* "For Emma, the abruptness was shattering, a sudden erasure of shared plans, closeness, and trust. The timing felt particularly wounding: it was as if Daniel had emotionally retreated to a life where Emma never truly belonged. In the weeks that followed, Emma struggled with questions: *Was I only a distraction? Was I never enough? Why couldn't he tell me sooner?*

Case Study Rudy and Sinead

Rudy and Sinead had been together for two years and had recently begun living under the same roof. For Sinead, the relationship was real, grounded in love, laughter, and the belief that they were building a future together. She had stood by Rudy with patience and understanding as he navigated life after loss. His late wife had passed several years earlier, and though Sinead knew there would always be a part of Rudy's heart that belonged to her memory, she believed there was space for her, too.

From the beginning, Rudy's home reflected the life he had shared before. Photos of his late wife, including intimate portraits, remained on display. Her jewellery was still in the bedroom, her perfume was on the dresser, and her clothes were hung neatly in the wardrobe. For a long time, Sinead didn't say anything. She didn't want to seem jealous of a woman who no longer existed in the physical world. But privately, it stung. Every time she reached for a drawer or passed a photo, she was reminded that she was living among relics of a love that once was.

Eventually, Rudy decided to pack away his late wife's belongings. For Sinead, it felt like a hopeful step, as though he was finally ready to make space for the life they could share.

They began talking about marriage, and for the first time, Sinead allowed herself to imagine a future that belonged to them both, not to the shadow of someone else's past. But just as things seemed to be moving forward, Rudy abruptly ended the relationship.

Rudy told Sinead he couldn't commit, that something "didn't feel right." His words were vague but final. He asked her to move out, insisting it was for the best. Sinead was blindsided, heartbroken, and confused. She couldn't understand how a man who had spoken about a shared future could suddenly retreat into emotional distance.

A few days later, Sinead returned to collect the last of her belongings. When she entered the house, her heart sank. The shelves and tables were once again filled with photos of Rudy's late wife. Her perfume sat proudly on the dresser. The jewellery box had been returned to its original place. It was as though Sinead had never existed.

For Sinead, the loss was twofold: she lost the man she loved, and she was also forced to witness him choose a ghost over her. Her heartbreak was not only about the end of the relationship but about the realisation that no matter how much love she gave, she could not compete with grief's grip on Rudy.

Case Study: Carla and Michael

Michael and Carla met on a cruise, and from the moment they locked eyes, the chemistry was undeniable. Their connection was instant, intense, and passionate, the kind of whirlwind that made Carla believe she had finally met "the one." The laughter, the late-night talks, and the gentle affection between them felt real and grounding. Carla found herself falling in love fast, swept up by the tenderness and attention Michael gave her.

After returning from the cruise, they saw each other almost every day. Michael mostly stayed at Carla's house, telling her he preferred being there because it felt "cosy and alive." Carla had only been to Michael's home briefly, to water his plants and collect some clothes for him. It was tidy and quiet, yet Carla noticed that it felt untouched, like time had stopped. Still, Carla didn't question it.

Carla had three cats, and she thought that was the reason Michael never invited her to stay at his place; she didn't want to leave her pets alone overnight, and perhaps he felt the same about her comfort. It never occurred to her that there might be another reason behind his reluctance.

When Carla realised she had fallen in love, she planned a beautiful evening dinner, wine, and a quiet movie at home. It was her way of opening her heart. Later that evening, she told Michael how she felt and asked gently if he felt the same. For the first time, his warmth vanished. He went quiet, his eyes distant. When Carla asked whether he saw a future with her, he avoided the question and quickly changed the subject. Confused, Carla tried to laugh it off, but the silence between them that night felt different, heavy, and uncertain.

The next morning, Michael kissed her on the cheek and said he needed to spend the day at home. Days passed, and her calls went unanswered. When he finally returned her message, his tone was cool and detached. He said he thought they needed "a break," explaining that things were "moving too fast." Carla was heartbroken, replaying every moment to figure out what she'd done wrong.

When they finally spoke, Carla asked him to be honest about his feelings. Michael said, *"My wife only died last year. I thought we were just having fun.* "Carla was stunned. She had known Michael was a widower, but she never realised how unhealed he truly was. Carla was devastated but determined to respect his space. Two months later, while out celebrating her friend's birthday at a busy club, she saw Michael cuddled up with another woman. Carla was devastated.

Recognising the Red Flags

Although each of these women, Emma, Sinead, and Carla, entered their relationships with hope and sincerity, their experiences reveal a shared emotional truth: loving an unhealed widower often means contending with grief that has not yet found its resting place. Each story is unique in circumstance, but together they illustrate the pattern of the *Widower's Fire*, that internal blaze of longing, guilt, and avoidance that can consume both the grieving man and the partner who tries to love him.

In Emma and Daniel's story, we see a widower whose heart still beats to the rhythm of anniversaries tied to the past. His re-wearing of his wedding ring and emotional withdrawal in the days leading up to his late wife's death anniversary show how anniversary reactions can reactivate unresolved mourning. As grief theorist J. William Worden explains, unprocessed grief can resurface cyclically, often triggered by dates or sensory reminders [38]. For Daniel, these triggers reignited feelings of loyalty and guilt, compelling him to retreat from Emma, even though she represented comfort and companionship.

Rudy and Sinead's story demonstrated a form of emotional retreat. Rudy's symbolic act of packing away his late wife's belongings briefly created the illusion of readiness to move forward. Yet when emotional intimacy deepened, his internal loyalty to his late wife re-emerged with force. As Pauline Boss describes in her theory of *ambiguous loss*, people like Rudy often live between two psychological worlds: the past relationship that still feels alive and the new relationship that demands emotional presence [12]. His re-displaying of his late wife's possessions after ending things with Sinead is a form of grief reclamation, an unconscious attempt to reaffirm a bond he fears losing by committing to someone new.

Carla and Michael's story reveals another dimension of the *Widower's Fire*, where grief manifests not through reminiscence but through physical and emotional substitution. Michael's pursuit of intimacy is a form of grief avoidance. According to professionals, mourners shift between confronting loss and avoiding it [39]. In some cases, avoidance takes the shape of compulsive attachment seeking, pursuing affection or sexual closeness not to connect, but to temporarily dull emotional pain.

For Emma, Sinead, and Carla, the common denominator is emotional exile. Each woman entered her relationship believing that empathy, patience, and love could help heal the past. Instead, she found herself competing with it. Their stories show how unhealed grief transforms relationships into battlegrounds between memory and reality. As grief scholar Alan Wolfelt notes, love after loss requires an active engagement with mourning, *not moving on but moving forward with grief* [39]. When this process is denied, the widower's new partner is unconsciously positioned as a threat to the deceased's legacy. Her presence triggers guilt rather than gratitude, comparison rather than connection.

The *Widower's Fire* can ignite quickly, creating passion, connection, and emotional intensity, but it is often unstable. When faced with the vulnerability of real intimacy, the widower's grief reignites. Some retreat, others lash out, and some seek new distractions. In every case, the result is emotional destruction. The partner is left carrying both her heartbreak and the widower's unprocessed sorrow.

From a professional lens, these stories remind us that love cannot heal what has not been acknowledged. A widower who has not made peace with his loss cannot offer stability to someone new. Until grief is named, felt, and integrated, every new relationship risks becoming another casualty of the fire. The *Widower's Fire* is not the warmth of love reborn, but the burning need to feel alive again, even if it means using another person's affection as fuel. Across this narrative, several core psychological mechanisms emerge:

1. **Ambiguous Loss and Continuing Bonds**. Each widower maintains a psychological connection with the deceased spouse, a bond that, when unintegrated, prevents the formation of secure emotional attachments. The new partner becomes the emotional outsider, witnessing but never sharing the sacred space of memory [12].

2. **Frozen Mourning and Symbolic Loyalty**. Many widowers unconsciously equate moving forward with betrayal. This *loyalty bind* can lead to emotional stagnation, where the widower protects his late wife's memory at the expense of his present partner's well-being [38].

3. **Avoidant Intimacy and Distraction Coping**. For some, romantic or sexual relationships provide a temporary escape from grief's intensity. Emotional numbing

masquerades as passion, but when the distraction fades, the unresolved sorrow resurfaces, often leaving the partner feeling used or discarded [39].

4. **Projection and Emotional Displacement**. Accusations of insensitivity or jealousy often mask the widower's own guilt or ambivalence. The partner becomes a scapegoat for feelings the widower cannot yet process [40].

Together, these stories show that loving an unhealed widower is not a failure of intuition, compassion, or worth on the part of the woman; it is the predictable consequence of stepping into a space where grief still rules the emotional landscape. The *Widower's Fire* feels bright and consuming at first, but without true mourning behind it, the flame cannot carry the weight of a real relationship. Women who enter these dynamics are not naïve; they are hopeful, generous, and often deeply empathetic. Yet no amount of care can substitute for the inner work a man has not done.

These narratives remind us that healing is not found in another person's arms but in a man's willingness to confront his loss. Until that happens, the woman who loves him is left contending not only with his past, but with the emotional fallout of a grief she did not cause and cannot cure. This chapter stands as both a caution and a comfort: what happened to Emma, Sinead, and Carla is not personal; it is structural, predictable, and painfully common. And by naming it, we give women the clarity, language, and strength to protect themselves before stepping into a fire that was never theirs to manage.

What to Remember

The *Widower's Fire*, the intense passion and emotion often seen in unhealed widowers, is not always love reborn, but grief unprocessed. Until that fire is understood and healed, it can consume both the widower and his new partner, turning what feels like a deep connection into emotional chaos and pain. True love cannot grow in the ashes of unresolved loss.

Chapter 28 – How to End the Relationship

"I felt that I was losing who I was as a person, I forgot to smile".

"Loving him hurt so much".

"I had no choice but to put myself first".

Sometimes, love alone isn't enough. You may care deeply for the widower you're dating, yet grief, family dynamics, or his unwillingness to invest in your shared future can keep the relationship stalled. Recognising this truth can be painful, even heartbreaking. But acceptance is not failure; it is an act of courage and self-respect.

For many women, the warning signs, or "Red Flags", of an unhealed widower are present from the very beginning, even if they can't fully put their finger on them. They simply sense that something isn't quite right.

In my own relationship with Bill, there were many Red Flag moments. One stands out vividly. Bill sat beside his late wife's shrine, speaking with conviction about how ready he was to move on and build a future with me. I looked at him and at the shrine, and I still didn't fully grasp that the answer was staring me in the face. I had no idea what I was stepping into when I fell in love with him.

I didn't consider myself a widow, though my previous partner had died of cancer. I thought I understood loss, grief, and love after death, until I met a man who called himself a widower. Bill's patterns were clear: he would withdraw in the weeks leading up to anniversaries and milestones connected to his past life. These actions felt like Red Flags, yet I pushed my feelings aside, caught in society's expectation that I should be endlessly compassionate about his loss. I told myself I needed to understand his grief, while my own heart quietly broke.

If you've had open conversations that lead nowhere, if your emotional needs are dismissed or belittled, if the relationship remains centred on his late wife with no space for new memories, and if you feel anxious, guilty, or lonely more often than loved and secure, these are serious signals. When efforts at compromise or therapy are met with anger, denial, or blame, it may be less about who you are and more about where he is on his healing journey.

Professionals remind us that healthy mourning allows space for new attachments. When a partner remains fully tethered to the past, there may simply be no emotional room for you, through no fault of your own [4]. Many women I have spoken with say it feels like living in the shadow of a ghost, constantly questioning their worth, doubting their perceptions, carrying a quiet sadness that never seems to lift.

Secure love is built on mutual care and respect. If that is persistently missing, your emotional well-being must come first [29]. If you find yourself living in the shadow of a ghost, the honourable and loving thing to do is choose yourself. Your peace, happiness, and sense of self are just as important.

Acceptance isn't resignation. It's choosing to live fully in the present rather than clinging to what cannot be changed [9]. Ask yourself: do I still feel hopeful about our shared future, or mostly tired? When we discuss difficult topics, does he respond with curiosity and care, or with defensiveness and blame? Am I becoming someone I don't like, anxious, self-doubting, endlessly accommodating? Sometimes the kindest choice for both people is to acknowledge that the relationship isn't ready to grow.

Reflect Before You Decide

Before making the difficult choice to leave, take a moment to look honestly at your experience. Ask yourself:

- Have I spoken up about my needs and given him a real chance to meet them?

- Am I prepared for the possibility that he may not fully understand, or be willing to acknowledge, why I need to step back?
- What is staying costing me emotionally, mentally, and spiritually?

Write down your answers. Seeing them on paper can help you distinguish between decisions made from hurt, fear, or guilt, and those rooted in clear self-awareness and respect for your own well-being.

Remember: choosing yourself is not failure. It is a courageous act of self-respect. Sometimes the most loving thing you can do, for yourself and for the relationship, is to step back, even when your heart still wants to stay.

Opening the Conversation

Ending a relationship with a widower can feel heartbreaking, even when you know it's the right choice. Speaking up isn't about blame; it's about honesty, self-respect, and protecting your emotional well-being. This is your chance to express clearly why you can no longer continue, while staying grounded in your truth.

Before you speak, take a moment to reflect on why you are stepping back. Consider:

- I feel unseen, unheard, or invisible. Is staying here costing me my sense of self?
- My needs are consistently ignored. Is this a partnership, or am I filling the space of someone from his past?
- I feel anxious, drained, or guilty more often than loved. Can I continue sacrificing my well-being for a relationship that doesn't meet me halfway?
- Conversations about the future are blocked or dismissed. Is he ready and able to build a life with me, or tethered to a past I cannot join?
- Milestones, holidays, and daily life revolve around his grief. Am I willing to live permanently in the shadow of a ghost?

Writing your answers down can help distinguish between decisions made from fear, guilt, or sadness, and those grounded in clear self-awareness and respect for your own needs.

Speaking Your Truth

When you open the conversation, focus on your experience and your boundaries, without debating his grief or intentions. Statements that are firm yet empathetic can include:

- "I feel invisible and anxious when our life is constantly overshadowed by your grief."
- "I need a relationship where my presence, feelings, and needs are equally valued, and that is not what I am experiencing here."
- "I have realised that I cannot continue this relationship and must step back to protect my emotional health."
- "This is not a judgment on your grief; it is about my own needs and boundaries."

Set clear boundaries for the discussion:

- Choose a calm, private setting, away from emotionally charged dates or anniversaries if possible.
- Keep the focus on your decision, not on debating his behaviour.
- Prepare emotional support afterwards, whether from a friend, family member, or counsellor.

Practical Steps Forward

Walking away from someone you love, especially a grieving widower, is not cruel. It is an act of courage, honesty, and self-respect. If you have supported the relationship, communicated your needs, and given it space to grow, but still feel invisible, undervalued, or emotionally depleted, it may be time to ask yourself: *Is this where my heart can truly thrive?*

If the answer is no:

- Have a clear, respectful conversation without blame.
- Prepare for mixed emotions: grief, relief, doubt, or sadness.

- Reconnect with your support system: friends, family, or a counsellor.
- Reflect on what you have learned about love, boundaries, and resilience.
- Allow yourself to grieve the relationship; it was real, even if it didn't last.

Checklist: Ending a Relationship

Ask yourself honestly:

- What am I afraid will happen if I leave?
- What do I hope might happen if I do?
- Which parts of myself have been quiet or hidden in this relationship?

Before stepping away, confirm you have:

- Reflected on your reasons and emotions.
- Spoken clearly about your feelings at least once, if possible.
- Chosen a calm, private moment for the conversation.
- Prepared to hold your boundary, even if he pleads, promises, or reacts emotionally.
- Created a plan for emotional support afterwards, friends, therapy or journaling.
- Reminded yourself that choosing to leave does not erase what was good; it honours your needs, growth, and well-being.

Ending a relationship with a widower is not failure, it is courage, self-respect, and prioritising your peace. Speaking your truth clearly and firmly is the first step in reclaiming your life, your voice, and your emotional safety.

What to Remember

Ending a relationship with someone still deeply attached to their late wife doesn't mean you were "not enough." It means you chose truth over hope alone and respected both his grief and your own need to be fully loved in the present. Letting go isn't giving up on love; it's making space for love that can meet you in the here and now. Leaving with kindness protects not just him, but your own heart, so it can remain open for what comes next.

Dear Me

I know how hard I tried. I walked into the relationship with open arms and an open heart, believing that love could heal grief, that patience and empathy would be enough. I thought that with enough tenderness, the shadows of the past would soften, and the two of us could build something beautiful in the present.

But it wasn't that simple, was it? I was never just loving *him*. I was loving *him and his past*, the late wife, the memories, the grief-soaked loyalty, the guilt he didn't speak of but never truly let go of. In trying to be understanding, I overlooked so much: the emotional withdrawal, the inconsistency, the long silences, and the growing sense that I no longer belonged in my own relationship.

I excused the mood swings, the blaming, the defensiveness. I told myself it was grief. Maybe I was being too sensitive. But deep down, I knew grief doesn't erase responsibility. Grief doesn't give someone permission to withhold love, use guilt as a weapon, or make me feel like I was asking too much for simply wanting to be chosen.

I didn't fail. I loved. That's never failure. I showed up fully, and when I realised that love was being met with avoidance, blame, or manipulation, I chose clarity over chaos. That's courage. I may never get closure from him, and that's okay. I am my own closure. I chose peace over confusion. I chose self-respect over being someone's emotional caretaker. I realised that real love doesn't make me beg for emotional crumbs.

Now it's my time to heal. To return to myself. To mourn not just the relationship, but the version of me that kept trying to earn love that should have been freely given. I'm not broken. I'm becoming, and in that becoming, I will build something stronger, not with someone who sees me as a replacement, but with someone who sees me as *enough*. Until then, I hold my heart gently. It's been through a lot. But it's still beating. And it still knows how to love. I now understand why living in the shadows of a ghost felt so cold. I've stepped back into the light, smiling at how good life can be. My heart is alive with possibility as I begin my next chapter, ready for love again, because life is for the living.

From Me

Relationship Reality Check

A guided way to understand the emotional landscape of your relationship. This checklist is intentionally layered, moving from how he sees himself, to his home, his grief patterns, the place his late wife still holds, your own emotional safety, and finally the future you may or may not be building together. Answer honestly and then check your answers in the next section, 'Interpreting your checklist'.

Answer Yes or No.

How He Sees Himself

These questions reflect his identity and readiness for a new chapter.

1. Does he describe himself as a widower rather than a single man building a new life?

2. Does he avoid talking about shared plans or next steps in your relationship?

3. Does he avoid conversations about living together, marriage, or blended family issues?

His Home, Environment, and Physical Space

Your surroundings reveal where emotional energy remains anchored.

4. Is the house largely unchanged, as though she might walk back in?

5. Are her photos, clothes, and mementos still displayed throughout the home?

6. Do I have to ask for space for my belongings or precious items?

7. Do I feel like an intruder when I try to make small changes in his home?

8. Does the home feel more like her space than our space?

His Grief Patterns and Emotional Availability

These questions show whether grief remains active and whether he has emotional room for you.

9. Does he continue to acknowledge anniversaries, birthdays, or dates connected to his late wife?

10. Does he still wear his wedding ring?

11. Does he find it difficult to talk about his late wife without becoming overwhelmed or closed off?

12. Do his moods dip sharply around significant anniversaries or milestones?

13. Do I feel unsafe or hesitant to express my needs?

14. Have I stopped asking for things that genuinely matter to me?

The Place His Late Wife Still Holds

This explores whether the past is honoured or overshadows the present.

15. Does he frequently talk about his late wife in idealised terms?

16. Does he say things like "She'd want this" instead of "I want this"?

17. Does he imagine a future with you, or primarily a future beside her memory?

18. Do I feel tolerated rather than chosen next to her memory?

19. Do his major life choices still seem guided by what his late wife would have approved of?

20. Does he speak about his late wife in ways that leave me feeling excluded?

21. Do I feel her presence in the relationship in ways I can't influence or discuss?

22. Do I feel like I am waiting for him to finish grieving, or being asked to wait?

Your Needs, Identity, and Emotional Safety

These questions clarify whether there is still room for **you** in the relationship.

23. Do I feel that my needs are regularly dismissed or overlooked?

24. Do I feel like I'm constantly proving my loyalty or worth?

25. Am I sacrificing my mental health to protect or "heal" his grief?

26. Would seeking outside support help me gain clarity about this relationship?

27. The relationship does not leave room for my interests, identity, and history?

28. Am I accepted as who I am, rather than how well I fit into his past life?

29. When I express discomfort, does he respond with defensiveness rather than empathy?

30. Do I feel emotionally unsafe or unseen in this relationship?

Shared Life, Future Plans, and Your Inner Knowing

These questions speak to your deeper truth.

31. Can I picture a future where we create new memories together?

32. When he suggests sharing hobbies or routines from his past, do I feel like I'm stepping into her role?

33. Do I feel guilty expressing my needs or emotions?

34. If nothing improved from this point forward, would I eventually feel unhappy staying?

35. Have I felt blamed or criticised for things I didn't do?

36. Am I giving myself permission to acknowledge
when something doesn't feel right?

Interpreting the Checklist: A Guide

This checklist is not meant to label your partner or declare a relationship "good" or "bad." Instead, it helps you understand **how much the past is shaping your present**, and whether you are being given the space, security, and emotional partnership you deserve.

Your "yes" answers reflect how much **the late wife, his grief, and his unresolved emotional patterns** are influencing the relationship.

Use this as a compass, not a verdict.

0–5 YES Answers

*The Past is Present, But Not Dominant***
If you're in this range:

- The late wife or past life appears in natural, understandable ways.
- You generally feel seen, valued, and included.

- You can talk about needs, boundaries, and the future without fear or guilt.
- His grief may surface, but it isn't steering the relationship.

You're likely not with an unhealed widower.
Normal communication, tenderness, and consistency are present.
Your relationship has room to grow.

6–12 YES Answers

*Past and Present Are in Tension***
This range suggests that the relationship is **carrying emotional mixed signals**:

- Parts of his life may still feel organised around the memory of his late wife.
- You may sense hesitation, avoidance, or emotional withdrawal at times.
- You might feel like you're trying to fit into a space that wasn't created for you.
- Conversations about the future may feel strained or unclear.

This doesn't mean he's unwilling, but it often means he's **not fully healed**.
You may need:

- an honest, grounded conversation,
- clearer boundaries,
- or reassurance that there is space for you in his life now, not later.

This is the "pay attention" zone. The relationship can grow, but not without clarity and change.

13+ YES Answers

*You May Be Loving an Unhealed Widower***
If many of your answers were "yes," you may be experiencing:

- A relationship still centred around the late wife rather than the living partner.
- An emotional home that hasn't been rearranged to include you.
- Grief that is still active, unresolved, or idealised.

443

- A pattern where your needs feel secondary, silenced, or invisible.
- A sense of living beside his past, rather than building a future together.

This level of impact often means you're carrying the emotional weight of his loss, while sacrificing parts of yourself to make the relationship work. This doesn't make you wrong or unloving. It simply shows that it might be time for a compassionate conversation or a courageous decision.

Your future, well-being, identity, and emotional safety matter.

Remember: trusting your instincts, noticing patterns, and protecting your emotional well-being is not a selfish act; it's necessary for a healthy and fulfilling life.

References

1. Kübler-Ross, E. (1969). *On Death and Dying*. Macmillan.

2. Kessler, D. (2019). *Finding Meaning: The Sixth Stage of Grief*. Scribner.

3. Keogh, A. (2011). *Dating a Widower: Starting a Relationship with a Man Who's Starting Over*. Ben Lomond Press.

4. Worden, J. W. (2018). *Grief Counselling and Grief Therapy: A Handbook for the Mental Health Practitioner* (5th ed.). Springer Publishing Company.

5. Stroebe, M., & Schut, H. (1999). *The Dual Process Model of Coping with Bereavement*

6. Keogh, A. (2014). *Dating a widower: Understanding grief, love, and new beginnings*. New York: HarperCollins.

7. Devine, M. (2017). *It's OK That You're Not OK: Meeting Grief and Loss in a Culture That Doesn't Understand*.

8. Elliott, D. (2009). *When a Man Faces Grief: 12 Practical Ideas to Help You Heal from Loss*. Willowgreen Publishing.

9. Boss, P. (2006). *Loss, Trauma, and Resilience: Therapeutic Work with Ambiguous Loss*.

10. Keogh, A. (2011). *Dating a Widower: Starting a Relationship with a Man Who's Starting Over*. Ben Lomond Press.

11. Elliott, S.J. (2009). *Getting Past Your Breakup: How to Turn a Devastating Loss into the Best Thing That Ever Happened to You*. Da Capo Press

12. Boss, P. (1999). *Ambiguous Loss: Learning to Live with Unresolved Grief*. Harvard University Press.

13. Keogh, A. (2011). *Dating a Widower: Starting a Relationship with a Man Who's Starting Over*. Ben Lomond Press.

14. Weiss, R. S. (1993). *Loss and recovery*. University of Chicago Press.

15. Field, N. P., & Filanosky, C. (2010). *Continuing bonds, risk factors for complicated grief, and adjustment to bereavement.* Death Studies.

16. Neimeyer, R. A. (2016). *Techniques of Grief Therapy: Creative Practices for Counseling the Bereaved.* Routledge.

17. Klass, D., Silverman, P. R., & Nickman, S. L. (1996). *Continuing bonds: New understandings of grief.* Taylor & Francis.

18. Humphrey, K. M., & Zimpfer, D. G. (2008). *Counseling for Grief and Bereavement.* Taylor & Francis.

19. Brubaker, J. R., Hayes, G. R., & Dourish, P. (2013). *Beyond the Grave: Facebook as a Site for the Expansion of Death and Mourning. The Information Society,*

20. American Psychiatric Association. (2022). *Diagnostic and Statistical Manual of Mental Disorders, Fifth Edition, Text Revision (DSM-5-TR).*

21. Malkin, C. (2015). *Rethinking Narcissism: The Secret to Recognizing and Coping with Narcissists*. HarperWave

22. Blackburn, P. (2016). *Widower's journey: Helping men rebuild after their loss*. Amazon Digital Services.

23. Rubin, S. S., Malkinson, R., & Witztum, E. (2012). *Working with the Bereaved: Multiple Lenses on Loss and Mourning*. Routledge.

24. Walter, T. (1999). *On bereavement: The culture of grief*. Open University Press.

25. Imber-Black, E. (1993). *Secrets in Families and Family Therapy*

26. Bowen, M. (1978). *Family Therapy in Clinical Practice*

27. Keogh, D. (2014). *When Your Spouse Dies: A Widow's Guide to Healing*. CreateSpace.

28. Keogh, A. (2011). *Dating a Widower: Starting a Relationship with a Man Who's Starting Over*. Ben Lomond Press.

29.   Bowlby, J. (1980). *Attachment and Loss: Volume III – Loss, Sadness and Depression*. Basic Books.

30.   Doka, K. J. (2002). *Disenfranchised grief: New directions, challenges, and strategies for practice*. Champaign, IL: Research Press.

31. Wolfelt, A. D. (2016). *Understanding Your Grief: Ten Essential Touchstones for Finding Hope and Healing Your Heart*. Fort Collins, CO: Companion Press.

32.   Meier, S., & Loss, G. (2013). *Grief, reward, and attachment: Neurobiological perspectives on bereavement and relationship intensity. Journal of Neuropsychology, 7*(2), 125–142.

33.   Field, N. P., Gal-Oz, E., & Bonanno, G. A. (2003). *Attachment, coping, and adjustment in bereaved spouses. Journal of Social and Personal Relationships, 20*(5), 579–594.

34. O'Connor, M. F., Wellisch, D. K., Stanton, A. L., Eisenberger, N. I., Irwin, M. R., & Lieberman, M. D. (2008). *Craving love? Enduring grief activates brain's reward center. NeuroImage, 42*(2), 969–972.

35. Goleman, D. (1995). *Emotional Intelligence: Why It Can Matter More Than IQ*. Bantam Books.

36. Bar-On, R. (2006). *The Bar-On model of emotional-social intelligence (ESI). Psicothema, 18*(Suppl), 13–25.

37. Eisenberger, N. I., & Lieberman, M. D. (2004). *Why rejection hurts: A common neural alarm system for physical and social pain. Trends in Cognitive Sciences, 8*(7), 294–300.

38. Worden, J. W. (2009). *Grief Counseling and Grief Therapy: A Handbook for the Mental Health Practitioner* (4th ed.). Springer.

39.   Stroebe, M., & Schut, H. (2010). *The Dual Process Model of Coping with Bereavement: A Decade On. Omega: Journal of Death and Dying,* 61(4), 273–289.

40.   Freeman, J. (2015). *Reconstructing Love after Loss: The Psychology of Romantic Relationships Post-Bereavement.* Routledge.

41.Kandel, E. R. (2000). *Principles of Neural Science* (4th ed.). McGraw-Hill.

42.   Bonanno, G. A., & Kaltman, S. (2001). *The varieties of grief experience.* Clinical Psychology Review, 21(5), 705–734.

43.   Schacter, D. L. (1996). *Searching for memory: The brain, the mind, and the past.* Basic Books.

44.   Doka, K. J. (2016). *Living with grief: Loss in later life* (5th ed.). Hospice Foundation of America.

45.   Kandel, E.R. (2006). *In Search of Memory: The Emergence of a New Science of Mind.* New York: W.W. Norton & Company.

46.   Listen to Give Grief a Chance Podcast - Give Grief a Chance. https://www.givegriefachance.com/listen/episode-199-witnessing-grief

47.   Stark, E. (2007). *Coercive Control: How Men Entrap Women in Personal Life.* Oxford University Press.

48.   Follingstad, D. R., & Rogers, J. L. (2013). *Psychological abuse and its consequences for mental health.* Journal of Family Violence, 28(2), 1–14.

49.   Post, J. M. (2015). *When Grief is Weaponized: Manipulation in Mourning.* Journal of Loss and Trauma, 20(5), 411–427.

50.   Walker, L. E. (2017). *The Battered Woman Syndrome: Effects of Prolonged Emotional Abuse.* Springer.

51. Herman, J. L. (1992). *Trauma and Recovery: The Aftermath of Violence from Domestic Abuse to Political Terror*. Basic Books.

52. Dutton, D. G., & White, K. R. (2013). *Narcissistic and manipulative traits in abusive relationships*. Aggression and Violent Behavior, 18(5), 512–520.

53. Hochschild, A. R. (1983). *The Managed Heart: Commercialization of Human Feeling*. University of California Press.

54. Elliott, S. J. (2013). *Surviving the Shadow of Loss: Emotional Consequences in New Relationships*. Family Process, 52(1), 56–72.

55. Bandura, A. (1977). *Social Learning Theory*. Prentice Hall. (for learned helplessness in relational contexts)

56. Dutton, M. A., & Goodman, L. A. (2005). *Coercion and trauma in intimate*

partner abuse. Violence Against Women, 11(12), 1423–1448.

57.   Follingstad, D. R., Coyne, L., & Gambone, L. (2016). *Emotional abuse and post-traumatic stress symptoms*. Journal of Interpersonal Violence, 31(13), 2183–2207.

58.   Stark, E. (2013). *Coercive Control: How Men Entrap Women in Personal Life* (expanded edition).

About the Author

Michele is a writer, truth-teller, and emotional truth seeker who writes with raw honesty about love, grief, healing, and the complexities of human connection. Drawing from her own deeply personal journey of loving and letting go of a widower, Michele brings voice to the unspoken heartbreak many women experience behind closed doors.

With compassion, clarity, and unwavering authenticity, Michele explores what it means to care deeply, hurt quietly, and ultimately rise with grace. Her work resonates with those navigating invisible pain, offering validation, reflection, and a gentle reminder that healing is not impossible.

Michele believes that our stories have the power to connect and awaken us. Through her words, she invites readers to reclaim their voice, honour their boundaries, and choose peace over confusion.

She is currently building a body of work that includes essays, videos and reflective guidance for women navigating life.